Voices on the Move

An Anthology by and about Refugees

Edited by Domnica Radulescu and Roxana Cazan

Solis Press

This book is dedicated to all immigrants, migrants, refugees, and people on the move.

Cover image: © Florinda Ruiz

Image credits: page 7t,b Wikimedia Commons; pages 10 and 11 © Florinda Ruiz; pages 13 and 14 © Santi Palacios; pages 45, 47 and 115 © Khaled Al-Maqtari; pages 51 and 65 © Eric Garcia; pages 148–53 and 155 © Claudia Bernardi.

ISBN: 978-1-910146-46-0

Published by Solis Press, PO Box 482, Tunbridge Wells TN2 9QT, Kent, England

Web: www.solispress.com | *Twitter:* @SolisPress

Contents

ESTRANGEMENT

VOICES

Acknowledgments

THE FIRST SPARKLE OF this book glistened into existence in June 2018, when Roxana and Domnica met each other for the first time at the Society for Romanian Studies Conference in Bucharest, Romania. Their similar exploration of the themes of exile and refuge in their creative work as immigrants and refugees themselves, as well as the kind of serendipitous life parallels that can occur when you live as a part of the global diaspora, led not only to a beautiful friendship but also to a fantastic collaboration on this volume. We are very grateful to Solis Press who decided unflinchingly to publish *Voices on the Move*, and to the editor Robert Gray, who worked tirelessly to meet all deadlines despite the global pandemic that has mangled our lives and schedules. We gratefully acknowledge the summer research Lenfest grants offered to Domnica by Washington and Lee University to support work on the anthology.

We would like to thank our contributors who had faith in our vision and worked diligently in the revision process and the final stages of readying the book for publication. The insights, the stories, the experiences, and the craft of their contributions give voice to a discourse about migration in a world where migrants, immigrants, and refugees are looked at with immense suspicion and fear. They demonstrate that we all share the same longings, dreams, and aspirations, regardless of where we were born or what life course we decided to follow. We are so grateful for their voices.

We also want to thank and acknowledge the presses, literary magazines, online platforms, and editors who allowed a reprint of some of the contributions included here. A list follows: Bull City Press, the University of Pittsburgh Press, *The Rumpus, Paris Review, Poets Reading the News, The New York Times*, VAC Poetry, FLF Press, Poets & Traitors, and femalefilmfestival.com.

We are also grateful to our families, who cheered us on as we were working on this book and made it possible for us to complete this project. In particular, we want to thank Milan, Ali, Nicholas, Alexander, and Henry. We thank you wholeheartedly, and we hope this book speaks to you as immigrants or descendants of immigrants yourselves. We love you to the moon and the sun and back.

It took us over a year and a half of putting this book together, and as we were completing it, a terrible pandemic swept over the world causing much death and suffering. Many refugees, particularly those stuck in no-man's-land or at borders or in *ad hoc* camps or in spaces ripe with abuse and violence, have been obliterated. As access to health care or to quarantine was extremely precarious to them, many lost their lives. The refugees that are being kept in inhumane conditions at the US borders have been forgotten even by the media as attention shifted to the development of the global pandemic.

Simultaneously, around the world, a series of protests began to call attention to racism and police violence against black people in the United States. Despite the threat of the pandemic, many people felt that it was time to speak up against racism and the unequal treatment of people of color. These protests have been triggered by the brutal murders of George Floyd and Breonna Taylor in Minnesota and Kentucky, respectively. These deaths are certainly not unique as we remember Atatiana Jefferson, Aura Roser, Stephon Clark, Philando Castille, Alton Sterling, Freddie Gray, Janisha Fonville, Eric Garner, Tamir Rice, Michael Brown, and the many others killed by the police in recent years. We are painfully aware of the extreme impact of a pandemic or of racism on those with the least resources and of our moral obligation as bystanders to respond. And we respond by listening to others. When we listen carefully, we hear the voices of those on the move.

Foreword

Ruth Behar

I AM WRITING AS THE apple and pear trees are flowering and slowly shedding their pearl-white petals. Spring arrives very late in Michigan, in the middle of May. This time of rebirth, desperately awaited, is always a joyful moment in the calendar, but now it is haunted by our long days of sheltering at home, days that are starting to feel unending during the relentless Covid-19 pandemic. I feel grateful, in a way I never have before, that I have a house in Michigan filled with things I have brought back from my travels in Spain, Mexico, and Cuba, where I was born. Now, unable to go anywhere, I am living in a house of memory, where things collected over the years bring back experiences from different times and places. And I am feeling, to my own surprise, differently about Michigan. I often say I live in Michigan, but I'm not from Michigan; it is not my home. But in the midst of the pandemic, something within me has softened. I have fallen in love with my house, and the trees that surround me, and feel gratitude for this nest.

We have been reduced to extreme helplessness in this amorphous time of the pandemic, feeling an intense awareness of our vulnerability as human beings. It is a historical moment of uncertainty, confinement, and fear, as an invisible "enemy," a virus, is ravaging lives everywhere. More than ever, we are seeing how interconnected we all are, no matter where we are. Everyone on the globe is in the same terrible situation of being both together and apart. In a deep poetic sense, we all now just have one home, the earth. But at the same time, we are anchored in very specific places, since one of the few effective things we can do to stay healthy is to restrict our interactions with other people and simply stay home, shelter at home, as we now say.

But what is home, and where is home, if you are a refugee at the border being kept in unsanitary and unacceptable conditions? What is home and where is home if you are an immigrant still traversing the sea or the desert, not sure yet where you will set down roots? What is home and where is home if you have settled in a place that still views you as a foreigner, as "undocumented," and therefore undeserving of calling that place where you live your home? What is home and where is home when you can't forget all those whom you lost in your old home to find freedom in a new home? And what is home and where is home if you are a woman who doesn't feel safe at home? Or if you are a child who has been orphaned by war, pestilence, and violence? And what is home and where is home if the tentacles of racism extend to every corner of society where they enforce policies and maintain attitudes that stand in the way of true diversity and inclusion? Are we willing to accept an idea of home built on inequality and injustice? Is that what we want home to be?

The book you are holding in your hands, *Voices on the Move*, offers responses to these questions in a multitude of genres: lyrical poetry, historical vignettes, personal stories, dramatic plays, and stunning images. Speaking both gently and fiercely, these voices open our hearts and minds to a fuller understanding of what it means to be unsettled, displaced, dispossessed, to be searching for a place to call home. In this time of the pandemic, when a recognition of our shared humanity is the only hope for our survival, the message of *Voices on the Move* is more urgent than ever. We must listen to the voices of refugees, and those who defend refugees, to learn how the yearning for a sense of belonging is a universal human desire, and to recognize that the need to have a home in which to shelter safely must become a universal human right.

As I read this book, I often thought back to the time I was ten and bedridden for a year. That was many decades ago, but the fears and uncertainties of those days are never far from my thoughts. We were immigrants recently arrived in New York from Cuba, and a car speeding on the other side of the Belt Parkway lost control, flew over the divider, and landed on the car right in front of us. The devastating accident took five lives. We were fortunate to survive—my parents, younger brother, grandmother, and me—but I was asleep in the back seat, and the impact of the crash led me to fall forward and fracture my femur. It was a bad break and I was placed in a body cast for a year. I couldn't move and my mother had to feed me, wash me, and bring me a bedpan. I was deprived of sunshine, outdoor play, and my friends. We had fled Cuba, and there I was, in a strange new land, still learning English, and completely immobile. If not for the compassion and empathy shown me by family, friends, neighbors, and medical caretakers, I would have stayed an invalid and not walked again. The awareness of my vulnerability changed me forever and made me the person I am today.

That is how I came to believe, as an anthropologist and a writer, that we must make ourselves vulnerable to understand the vulnerability of others. Among the most vulnerable today are displaced and migrant people from all corners of the world. The plight of those in such a dire situation is described powerfully by Marjorie Agosín in *"Tristeza*/Sadness" (page 16), one of her three poems in this volume, as "Sadness of shadows/The sadness of absence/The sadness of those without a country."

Domnica Radulescu and Roxana Cazan, the devoted editors of this book, seek to awaken compassion and empathy for those searching for home, those who are lacking the essential freedom of being able to say, "Here is my house, here are my flowering trees." Read this book and take the stories shared here into your own life. If each of us, in our own way, can add just a grain of sand to this conversation, I am certain we can make the world a place where we all share one home on our beloved earth while we shelter safely in our *casitas* and dream at night without fear for tomorrow.

Introduction

Voices on the Move is a collection of diverse artistic works ranging from poetry to creative fiction and nonfiction, from drama to photography. The collection is inspired by the multilayered experience of displacement, with a focus on the migration of what Edward Said calls "large aggregates of humanity" of the last several decades. Most of the contributors to the collection are themselves immigrants or refugees to the United States or Western Europe and/or have been closely involved and worked with displaced peoples, such as migrants unfairly kept in detention centers or struggling to resettle in the host country. This fact offers a heightened level of authenticity and truthfulness to the collection. Although not all the works emerge from the most recent realities of immigration or reflect directly the devastation caused by the political climate that has emerged since 2016, they all process these realities through the lens of the present climate as gestures of resistance and denunciation.

The multifaceted artistic exploration of the trauma of migration unfolds with a sense of urgency that engages and awakens readers to the harsh realities faced by millions as they escape war, famine, and gang violence only to encounter new and unexpected difficulties in the countries where they have asked for refuge, in particular in the United States and in Western European nations. This book could not be more relevant and necessary today, having arisen as a direct and impassioned response to the present realities of the migration of peoples, in the belief that artistic expression in all its forms has the power to transform, heal, raise consciousness, and incite to real action in the world.

Voices on the Move reflects the realities of refugee life that have become particularly problematic after the United States announced its Executive Order 13769, also known as "the travel ban," and the Trump Presidency declared its zero-tolerance attitude towards undocumented immigrants, particularly those arriving from Mexico or Central and South America. This anthology represents our protest against racist injustice, oppression, fearmongering, murder, and hatred that have become all too frequent in the US, the UK, and other Western countries, phenomena which rekindle some of the darkest moments in history, from the genocides of native populations, to slavery, to the multifarious evils of colonialism and white supremacy. Such political violence affects millions of refugees, particularly as many of them identify or are labeled as people of color. As such, this multi-genre anthology is not only concerned with border crossings, but also with the ways in which migration, refuge, and exile issue a creative space in which the voices of those engaged in movement can be heard.

★ ★ ★

The executive order issued by US President Donald Trump on January 27, 2017 suspending entry of all refugees to the United States for 120 days triggered a massive reaction. Syrian refugees already confined to temporary camps such as the famous Za'atari camp in Jordan or the short-lived "Calais jungle" in France, were indefinitely blocked from seeking asylum in the USA. Citizens of seven largely Muslim countries were also prevented from entering the United States for 90 days. Although a federal appeals court rejected the initial presidential ban, a revised March 2017 injunction continued targeting these individuals. In April 2018, the Trump administration's family separation policy was officially passed as a means of deterring undocumented immigrants from entering the country along the US–Mexico border. As a result, US federal authorities separated children from the guardians who accompanied them in the United States, attracting virulent international criticism. Despite the issuance of an injunction against the family separation policy in June of the same year, in early 2019 the Trump administration acknowledged that many children continue to remain separated from their families with no plan of reunification.

As a result of these catastrophic events and the general unease surrounding migration in the twenty-first century, writers began responding with visceral literary and artistic accounts of their experiences with immigration and exile. For instance, Pakistani novelist Mohsin Hamid's *Exit West* (Riverhead Books, 2017) features a refugee couple seeking shelter in a post-apocalyptic West by escaping a war-torn country via a series of magical doors; Lauran Markam's *The Far Away Brothers* (Random House, 2018) follows the story of Salvadoran twins who escape poverty and fight to survive and belong in California, USA; and Syrian-American Osama Alomar's *The Teeth of the Comb & Other Stories* (New Directions, 2018) captures the mood of a people stifled under a harsh regime. Poetry such as Aracelis Girmay's collection *The Black Maria* (BOA, 2016) and Ocean Vuong's collection *Night Sky with Exit Wounds* (Copper Canyon, 2016) similarly highlights the harrowing experience of immigration and seeking acceptance in the host community. Cartoonists such as Eric Garcia, a contributor in our anthology, Riham El-Hour, or the elusive

Banksy contribute to the global immigration and asylum-seeking discourse in unrelentingly critical ways that shed light on global political decisions and policy makers.

Apart from individually published art and literature, anthologies of writing by and about refugees, immigrants, and asylum seekers have begun to demand renewed national and international attention. For instance, in April 2018, Harry N. Abrams published Viet Thanh Nguyen's edited collection entitled *The Displaced: Refugee Writers on Refugee Lives.* The anthology collects essays written by refugee writers about refugee life. Despite their global perspectives given their diverse circumstances and journeys, the contributors depict a shared trauma as they discuss the harrowing experiences of separation, uncertainty, resilience, and an enduring sense of identity. They also embody a distinct cohort: from MacArthur Genius grant recipients, National Book Award and National Book Critics Circle Award finalists, filmmakers, and lawyers, to professors and journalists. Joyce Carol Oates writing in *The New Yorker* called Nguyen "one of our great chroniclers of displacement."

The introduction of Nikesh Shukla and Chimene Suleyman's edited collection *The Good Immigrant: 26 Writers Reflect on America* published by Little, Brown & Co. in early 2019 reads, "The title was a response to the narrative that immigrants are 'bad' by default until they prove themselves otherwise. They are job stealers, benefit scroungers, girlfriend thieves, and criminals. Only when they win an Olympic medal, treat you at your local hospital, or rescue a child from the side of the building do they become good." In a way, this book echoes the message Viet Thanh Nguyen put forth almost a year earlier, through compelling essays that devote space to subjects with which society is struggling to come to terms.

Another comparable publication comes from Olive Branch Press in March 2019. *Making Mirrors: Writing/Righting by and for Refugees* is "a poetry anthology that illuminates exile and displacement" as the book cover announces, and is edited by Palestinian poet and aid worker Jehan Bseiso and US-based poet Becky Thompson. By contouring a poetics of belonging, the poems included problematize the refugee/citizen binary as they also shape up exile as a creative space. While all contributors have a strong connection to the Middle East, a number of them reflect on the Mediterranean passage as a traumatic journey and depict the Mediterranean Sea as a burial site. Another anthology of poetry is Patrice Vecchione and Alyssa Raymond's stunning *Ink Knows No Borders: Poems of the Immigrant and Refugee Experience* published in 2019 by Seven Stories Press. The collection contains 64 poems that confront life after relocation.

In May 2018, Random House published *A Country of Refuge: An Anthology of Writing on Asylum Seekers,* edited by former director of English PEN's Writers in Prison Committee from 1991 to 2006, the Romanian-British Lucy Popescu. British and Irish writers, the contributors write stories of asylum seeking in Britain at a time when Brexit debates accentuated the negative press given those seeking a safe haven in the UK. Like *A Country of Refuge, Refugees and Peacekeepers* is a Patrician Press anthology of poems and short stories published in January 2017 that started as a writing contest organized by the British press. These books' main focus is on Britain and the ways in which British contemporary politics enable a dialogue about immigration.

The Australian collection, *Home Truths: An Anthology of Refugee and Migrant Writing,* edited by Yannick W. Thoraval and Caroline Petit, was published by Yannick Thoraval in 2015. Refugees and migrant writers from Africa and Asia, the contributors share their experiences with war and marginalization in the context of Australia's feeble tolerance of indigenous peoples and asylum seekers. The representation of the human desire for connection and building meaningful relationships foreshadows the message of *We Refugees,* another Australian project from Pact Press which is forthcoming.

Clearly, the topic of migration in all its forms continues to puzzle writers and readers alike. *Voices on the Move* comprises multi-genre literature written by and about refugees about the process of seeking refuge, its aftermath, and its impact on the body politic. As we tried to illustrate through its title, the collection overall is concerned with the issue of borders, security, identity, and voice. Like those before it, this anthology constitutes only a line of notes in the splendid chorus that is multicultural literature.

★ ★ ★

The works of art gathered in this collection, whether in the form of lyric or narrative poetry, creative fiction, creative nonfiction, dramatic monologues, theater, photography, or graphic art form a carefully woven and colorful tapestry held together by the unifying thread that is the yearning and search for real or imaginary places of belonging. The contributions are delicately poised on the line between loss and recovery, traumatic displacements and reinvention of hospitable landscapes. Many of the works stretch across the confluence between the devastation of recent wars and the immense waves of migration and displacement caused by them. These recent wars—such as the Syrian War—harken back to a recent history of genocide and trauma that inflects the current discourses of displacement and tints the public perception of immigration and refuge. If as has been said, post-traumatic stress disorder is a "disorder of memory" in Cathy Caruth's clinical terms, many of the works collected here explore such disorders, recover and turn memory into a valuable receptacle of experience, of lost spaces and wounded selves in search of healing.

The works are gathered thematically around four main ideas that constitute the four main parts of the anthology: "Waterways" challenges the reader to understand enforced migration as a kind of drowning, literal and figurative, of one's original identity and self-awareness. "Journeys" paints a map of migration routes that poses similar threats and challenges regardless of who committed to following it. "Estrangement" points to the sacrifices and traumas all those seeking refuge encounter in different ways. Finally, "Voices" considers the ways in which migrants have access to telling their own stories of displacement.

Several of the poems included here capture delicate encounters between the displaced self and the natural elements to connect to that which is permanent and transcends location. Others focus on nature as a tomb for refugees such as the waters of the Mediterranean that have swallowed so many in their desperate crossings as in "Upon Realizing There Are Ghosts in the Water" (Chatti). Like Chatti's, Moscaliuc's poems paint a staggering picture of a personal immigration trauma that recalls memories of oppression during a totalitarian regime. The poetic languages created here oscillate from elegant simplicity:

> When we talk about migrants
> We should breathe more and talk less.
> But if we must talk, we should speak
> in the language of water. (Peterson, page 157)

to raw and stridently colored imagery of grief and violence:

> Each line is arrowed red.
> Inside, they tumble
>
> across muscled continents
> like erythrocytes, millions
>
> of flesh-tucked skulls hauling
> the heaviness of dreams. Red for departure,
> blue for return. (Metres, page 56)

If Agosín's poetic work echoes the tradition of *testimonio* written by Latin American women, Cazan's poetic work departs from traditional form and engages in experiment as a means of reflecting the trauma of exile. In the essay accompanying her poems, Cazan invites the reader to consider the healing power of poetry to mitigate the threat or the fear of cultures one knows very little about. While Lockhard's poetry reminds the reader of the first refugees on the North American continent, Hada's work points the finger to some of those who continue the colonizing mission of the imperial era.

The creative fiction tells wrenching stories of departures and farewells and delves into the "disorder of memory" of resettling refugees, their desperate yet stubborn struggles to resettle, re-root, and belong. They often move in fractured narratives of a hyphenated present and haunting flashbacks, as in the story of a young Nepalese refugee titled "Miss Me Forever," or glide in nostalgic ripples as they reinvent buried pasts and reconsider the present possibility of a returning to a war-torn country as in Lana Spendl's "Geography of Peaks, and Dips, and Lights." Bárbara Mujica's short story "Sanchez across the Street" beautifully unravels yet another facet of immigrant lives as it depicts the startling confrontations between different communities of immigrants, in this case a Jewish family with a history of Holocaust victims and a newly arrived Mexican family with many children. Although set during the Vietnam War era, the set of prejudices, cultural clashes, misunderstandings, and tragic outcomes are entirely comparable to today's landscapes of immigrant realities.

Radulescu's bilingual play "*Bienvenus à la jungle de Calais*/Welcome to the Jungle of Calais" emerged from stories of refugees, undocumented migrants, and asylum seekers from African and Middle Eastern countries in the former Calais camps in northern France. Using shape shifting and Brechtian techniques of epic theater, the play unfolds as an artistic testimony to the wrenching journeys and water crossings of migrants desperately trying to settle in Western Europe. Like Radulescu's, Cristina Bejan and Catalina Florescu's dramatic contributions also employ bilingualism as they explore journeys of estrangement and identity formation or reclaiming. Their short plays help the reader understand that despite the different chronotopes, the characters seek to escape similarly oppressive realities that stifle them.

The creative nonfiction pieces are poised on the line between art production and the upholding of human rights for members of those "large aggregates of humanity." In her cross-genre piece "Human Cries Keep Falling Like Summer Rain," Florinda Ruiz performs a vibrant *tour de force* of placing the unstoppable waves of migrants crossing the Mediterranean in recent years within the historical perspective of war and displacement of the Iberian Peninsula as recorded and channeled in both major works of visual art as well as in her own poetry and stunning photography. Claudia Bernardi's essay *"La Bestia/*The Beast: A Visual Investigation of the Journey of Undocumented Unaccompanied Central American Minors Crossing the Mexico–United States Border," deriving from her art therapy work with unaccompanied, undocumented minors from Mexico and Central America, kept in detention centers in the United States, brings out with great poignancy the power of creative expression as a strategy of survival and hope. Both Jasmin Darznik and Elizabeth Eslami write about living as Iranian-Americans, at a time when this particular existence is made precarious by the possibility of an impending war. In light of their own traumatic experiences of displacement, both Darznik and Eslami challenge preconceived ideas of home all the while fiercely holding on to a hope, a dream, and a possibility of one.

The visual works gathered in this collection, whether in the form of the sharply ironic cartoons "El Machete Illustrated," the intense and deeply mindful photographs of Yemeni refugees in Djibouti camps by Khaled Al-Maqtari or Florinda Ruiz's stark and breathtaking photographic moments of "Maritime Massacre" speak for themselves and give the collection its colorful multidimensionality as well as its edge of authenticity.

As editors of the book and creative artists, we hold on to the hope that *Voices on the Move* will awaken compassion and understanding of the unimaginable realities faced by displaced and migrant people from all corners of the world, educate, move, and potentially incite to action towards the defense of human rights and social justice. And as both immigrants and writers, we believe in the power of the personal story and in the illuminating force of art to tell the deepest truths about the traumas of loss and exile, and equally to create homes and spaces of belonging. This book is yet another attempt to grapple with unearned privilege as we aim to connect with others who do not have privilege but share deeply in our humanity.

Domnica Radulescu and Roxana Cazan

Waterways

Human Cries Keep Falling Like Summer Rain

Florinda Ruiz

> Sing, goddess, the rage of Pelias' son Achilles,
> its devastation, that gave the Achaeans endless pain
> and hurled many brave souls of heroes to Hades—
> while it made their bodies a delicate feast for dogs
> and all birds, as Zeus' will was fulfilled. (*The Iliad*, 1–5)

> The first time it was reported that our friends were being butchered there
> was a cry of horror. Then a hundred were butchered. But when a thousand
> were butchered and there was no end to the butchery, a blanket of silence
> spread. When evil doing comes like falling rain, nobody calls out "stop!"
> When crimes begin to pile up they become invisible. When sufferings
> become unendurable, the cries are no longer heard.
> The cries, too, fall like rain in summer.
> (Bertolt Brecht. Translation from *Poems 1913–1956*, edited by John Willett
> and Ralph Manheim)

THE ENDLESS WARRING OF humankind and horrific loss of life repeats itself throughout civilizations, centuries, and continents as a permanent failure of humanity. Intolerance, like rain, might be dormant or quietly simmer at times, until an eventual surge of seething foam flares up and smothers the fate of entire civilizations or smaller human groups by subjugating, victimizing, slaughtering, and vanquishing the most vulnerable individuals. Human cleansing always occurs in the name of a higher call, be it a god of religion, a "superior" political ideology, or a combination of greed and economic interests.

Why are we to sing the rage of Pelias' son or the fulfillment of Zeus' treacherous will? Why not speak the voice of their butchered recipients and lift the blanket of silence? The world has lived and relived that inherited rage throughout centuries on end, across ages and continents. In the Mediterranean, one of those lands has been Iberia—an invaded land, a land of invaders, a nation of conquerors and conquered peoples, a site of dictatorships and revolutions, a mix of peoples who have defended their particular beliefs, yet fought to impose them on vulnerable others. Refugees have departed from and flocked into this land at the crossroads of oceans and seas, continents and races, empires and republics, dictators and monarchs, conquistadors and revolutionaries, captives and slave-owners, fascists and communists, dream catchers and dream smashers. From Hamilcar and Hannibal's Carthaginian conquests onto Hispania in 237BC and the siege of Iberian natives by Romans in Numantia in 133BC to the deadly risks undertaken today by African migrants escaping war and poverty to enter Europe, Iberia remains permanently linked to the constant struggle of imposed human displacements both in its peninsular territories and overseas.

Our last names, *Muley*, *Samur*, *Benjumea*, *Salama*, *Rabal*, or *Medina*—reminders of a negated, thus forgotten existence—still echo the losers' tragic lot in the clash between Christian and Islamic cultures. Those surnames retell the Moors' final expulsion from the peninsula in 1609. As depicted by Pere Oromig's 1616 painting, "Departure of Moriscos from Valencia's Port" (Figure 1, page 7), the first royal decree of expulsion resulted in harsh deportations by sea, mostly towards Oran and Tremecén in Africa. About 300,000 Spanish Muslims were expelled from Spain. Their children, separated from their parents, were kept in the peninsula to be raised by priests as Christian servants or work for Spanish prelates and noble families. The influx of thousands of stateless refugees from Spanish ports soon became too difficult to handle by African cities like Oran; sadly, many Spanish Muslims fell victims of violent hostilities on North African shores, as illustrated by Vicente Mestre's 1613 contemporaneous depiction of the calamities (rapes, murders, thefts, etc.) that refugees suffered on arrival to Oran's coasts (Figure 2, page 7).

But the seething foam of intolerance toward Muslims and Jews as "the others" had begun to simmer in the peninsula five centuries earlier. Already in 1267, the Andalusi poet Abū al-Baqā' ar-Rundī's elegy records the profound despair for and sorrowful resignation on the looming destiny of the fallen Spanish Muslim cities after the first century of cleansing deportations and forced evictions:

> Ask Valencia what became of Murcia,
> And where is Játiva, or where is Jaén?
> Where is Córdoba, the seat of great learning,
> And how many scholars of high repute remain there?
> And where is Seville, the home of mirthful gatherings
> On its great river, cooling and brimful with water?
> These cities were the pillars of the country:
> Can a building remain when the pillars are missing?

The white wells of ablution are weeping with sorrow,
As a lover does when torn from his beloved:
They weep over the remains of dwellings devoid of Muslims,
Despoiled of Islam, now peopled by infidels!
Those mosques have now been changed into churches,
Where the bells are ringing and crosses are standing.
Even the mihrabs weep, though made of cold stone,
Even the minbars sing dirges, though made of wood!
Oh heedless one, this is fate's warning to you:
If you slumber, Fate always stays awake.

More than five centuries have now passed. What has humankind learned? Has the modern world changed? Lushootseed Chief Seattle's speech offered in 1854 a similar and personal answer at the concession of his native lands to North American settlers:

There was a time when our people covered the whole land, as the waves of a wind-ruffled sea cover its shell-paved floor. But that time has long since passed away with the greatness of tribes now almost forgotten [...] Your God loves your people and hates mine; he folds his strong arms lovingly around the white man and leads him as a father leads his infant son, but he has forsaken his red children; he makes your people wax strong every day, and soon they will fill all the land; while my people are ebbing away like a fast-receding tide, that will never flow again. The white man's God cannot love his red children or he would protect them. They seem to be orphans and can look nowhere for help [...] It matters but little where we pass the remainder of our days. They are not many. The Indian's night promises to be dark. No bright star hovers about the horizon. Sad-voiced winds moan in the distance. Some grim Nemesis of our race is on the red man's trail, and wherever he goes he will still hear the sure approaching footsteps of the fell destroyer and prepare to meet his doom, as does the wounded doe that hears the approaching footsteps of the hunter.
Chief Seattle, "The Chief Seattle's Speech"[1]

The well-seasoned, flawed, DNA gene of human intolerance resurfaces as a common denominator in all nations and ages with different degrees of intensity and "nuance" through its repeated stages: subjugation, blame on the subjugated body for the mere sin of being, invalidation of a group's culture and beliefs, limited offer to become a second-

---

[1]   Translated from the Lushootseed language by Dr. Henry A. Smith and published as "Early Reminiscences. Number Ten. Scraps from a Diary. Chief Seattle – A Gentleman by Instinct – His Native Eloquence. Etc., Etc." *Seattle Sunday Star,* October 29, 1887, p. 3.

class member of the triumphant society, dehumanization, and exile or destruction.

New versions and methods of human massacre have continued to unfold. Since 2014, the Missing Migrants Project (MMP) began to systematically record deaths on migration routes worldwide. So far, MMP has recorded 30,602 deaths, likely a much higher number considering the challenges of collecting information about undocumented migrants and refugees. In 2015, about a million people risked their lives crossing the Mediterranean to reach Europe. As one of the world's deadliest sea-crossings, the Mediterranean hit a record high number of migrants' deaths with close to 5,000 in that one year, according to the UN Refugee Agency, UNHCR. In only five years, a minimum of 15,000 migrants and refugees (half of the world's total migrant death toll recorded by MMP since 2014) have lost their lives at Mediterranean sea-crossings, risking everything to access a sliver of personal dignity and hope. Based in Spain, the non-governmental organization Open Arms (www.openarms.es) provides first aid to migrants in the Mediterranean by remaining at sea with a rescue and surveillance boat. They are determined to not leave a single life adrift and have rescued 60,515 people from 2015 to 2020. The migrants they save are not numbers, but humans with a story and a voice, who find themselves in one of the most dangerous voyages of their lives. However, even as a member of the International Maritime Rescue Federation, despite numerous international awards, nongovernmental organizations such as Open Arms depend on small contributions from private individuals and are constantly fighting to try to preserve human rights at sea. Can European officials hear the cries of horror, lift the blanket of inaction, and muster the organizational humanity to save lives?

The burden of oppression is carried on the shoulders of nameless people, jailed and killed ancestors, enslaved by the color of their skin, targets of religious persecution, bastions of resistance, executed by firing squads, enslaved in transatlantic lands, expelled to unknown territories, often simply lost and forgotten in folds of blankets of silence. The echoes of their suffering bounce from the hinges and joints of altered history school-books, to ignored corners of our museums' greatest paintings and treasures. As testimonies of ethnic, religious, and political cleansings, their memories, in search for a voice, peak at us from dusty family photographs and treasured jail letters, from torn posters of war propaganda and quiet voices of unrecorded family conversations, from the aching backs of child workers and the hurting bodies of crowded immigration centers, from the anonymous images of frail migrant faces in our daily newspapers.

As victims are often obscured by the mythology and manipulation of the victors' corpulent regimes, poems forge a posthumous remembrance of the lives and sentiments of the inaudible fallen. Intolerance, abject poverty, discrimination, or war are not simply the backdrops of each poem, but the active staging elements that manifest the human tragedy of actual victims, their fears, carnage, hopes, or endurance. Poems bear witness to lost and silent voices, to words that were drowned, burnt or hidden, to their shattered lives or limitless resilience. The gap of thought between the visual and the verbal is bridged today by the power of the photographer's testimony. The combined tool of poetry and image can expand and share the emotional experience of an object, subject, place, or event with qualities that go beyond the physical aspects of an initial image; a way to step into human conflicts and inhabit the subjects and realities that surround us. The synergic blend of images and words engages with the idea that exists behind a visual representation of reality (Figures 3 and 4, pages 10 and 11). An image could be worth a thousand words, but poems can be the result of thousand images. They are verbal collages inserted in "multiple-exposure" verses: poetic reflections on the background, reconstructions of shattered beings, political turmoil, prejudice, and profound emotions that shape and ground subjects, images, and our own viewing act. Some of those connections are triggered by the committed and globally awarded work of Spanish photojournalists such as Santi Palacios (Figures 5 and 6, pages 13 and 14). His stunning body of humanitarian work, a story of migration, emerges from a dedicated field presence at the deadly center of dangerous migratory routes and conflicts.

We must engage both ethically and aesthetically with the experience of the suffering of others, stretching the canvas, the lens, the language, and our thoughts to evoke and converse with the saddened spirit of the image. In doing so, poems can search for necessary or avoided questions, forgotten or ignored realities, and underlying or unspoken truths. I wish to rescue invisible voices from blankets of silence, to spread the cries of their sufferings beyond the quiet falling summer rain.

> Our mission, therefore, is to confront ignorance with knowledge, bigotry with tolerance, and isolation with the outstretched hand of generosity.
> Kofi Annan

FIGURE 1 Departure of Moriscos from Valencia's port. Pere Oromig, 1616.

FIGURE 2 Arrival of Moriscos to Oran. Vincent Mestre, 1613.

Poem #1

Moriscos 1609

Forbidden faith.
Banned language.
Hands of henna, outlawed.
Our names, dropped.
Our rituals, banished.
   Abolished identity.

Forced were our baptisms.
Obliged to recite by heart
someone else's prayers.
Conversos, Marranos, Moriscos. We.
Nothing was quite enough
to erase our difference.

Our blood, one-drop,
an insubordinate aberration,
the stubborn otherness of birth.
Barred from our homes,
scattered through Iberia
as felons for mere being.

Suspicions, trials, and murders spiraled.
   Hunted
strangers in our torn apart world,
once the backbone of a country's wealth,
now vulnerable and helpless.
   Cursed.

Not a danger to the crown's empire,
nor a threat to the monolith of its faith.
Prey to the zeal of purging.
   Limpieza de sangre.

A secret fleet of Spanish galleons
awaited, hidden, just for us.
"Heretics, apostates, and traitors",
read the Royal Decree of expulsion.
Three days notice to removal,
Three days notice to departure,
Three days notice to a last farewell,
Three days notice to forsake our children,
Three days notice to never return to our land.

Dumped on African shores,
robbed, raped, ravaged.
Surviving on hopes of returning
to our abandoned *mihrabs,*
living on broken vestiges
of Andalusian memories.

Our blood still dwells
   in altered Spanish names.
Our worth remains
   in each city's bricks and pillars.
Our treasures are buried
   in the mosaic walls of a country's
   consciousness.

Sing now the richness of our souls,
a memory to all victims of bigotry.
Spanish Muslim exiles,
   Andalusíes.

Poem #2

Maritime Massacre

Dreams of food, water, survival,
a mother pushing him northwards.
She pressed, she prodded,
"no militias, no lynchings, my boy".
A crossing hope away from their inferno.

She imagined for him the colors of our side.
"Flee!"
And her only son took the northbound trail.
A journey of countless humans,
a tall order of endurance and discovery:
the exploits of a black conquistador,
black pilgrim, black cowboy, black astronaut,
the defiance of a black Herakles' heart.

The yoke of smugglers.
The toll of debt-bondage.
The threat of slave-markets.
The ramshackle prison camps.
The perilous sea crossing.
The final maritime choke point.
Worthy trials for a black young man's formidable labors.

A dinghy stuffed, 130 crowded hopes,
a squalid unseaworthy vessel,
bearing the wary spirits of waterless lands
scarred by the onslaught of starvation,
launching to fight dragons in our moat's waters.
He braved his fears into the monsters' deep wide trench,
our fluid deterrence to his human dare of crossing.

The news: "Another ravaged boat
has washed up on a European coast."

His infinite silence haunts her now
with tears attached to an everyday naming him.
She cannot know …

if his bold dreams capsized in the liquid cemetery,
if his hands held someone as the fosse welcomed them,

if his tears blended with the sea or dried in the sand,
if his shirt's wet wrinkles lie forgotten on some shore,

or maybe a rescuer found a living minute

to ask his name and touch him,
to hear a final sound from his breathless world,
to save a glimpse of the rhythms of his land,
to watch a wave erase the last footprint of his heroic intent.

FIGURE 3 African Herakles. Photograph by Florinda Ruiz.

FIGURE 4 Herakles and the anchor. Photograph by Florinda Ruiz.

Poem #3

Left Behind

Sheltered by sands in random dark beaches,
capsized remains of star-crossed
dinghies.
Scattered through seashores,
sodden mementos of landings and
wrecks.

Smothered life jackets
of sunken dead bodies.

Orphaned identities
of passports adrift.

Smudged blurry scribbles
of soaked weary booklets.

Cramped Qur'an verses
of voiceless sad prayers.

Cloaked by the foam of ancient white caps,
forgotten old trophies from toppled
chimeras.
Scavenged by waves in hidden mute coves,
as salvaged treasures of dreaming
skeletons.

Unspoken. Unwritten. Unsung. Unheard.
Unknown tombless names engraved in the water.
Liquid shrines to unreturning dead.

FIGURE 5 Migrants' belongings series. © Photographs by Santi Palacios.
Clockwise from top left: life-jacket; booklet; page from the Qur'an; passport.
Support for the inclusion of Santi Palacios' © photographs in this book was
provided by the Class of 1956 Provost's Faculty Development Endowment at
Washington and Lee University.

Poem #4

Perched

Six meters high
triple-layered fence
of metal righteousness,
blades of white virtue
running its length,
spotlights' tall pickets,
and cameras' posts.

A hazardous border,
splashed by sea waves
and African hopes,
awaiting and hiding
in makeshift camps.
Alert to a miracle moment,
the touch-and-go instant,
the razor-wire climb,
the fast jump to Europe.

And now, you,
perched, pensive,
stretching your life's seconds,
never this high,
never this view,
never this close,
a king above your own dream
atop the world,
atop the waves,
atop the white men's ways.

Not yet ready for the catch
but for wings
to surrender into the air
to glide to your freedom
as a petrel or a shag,
as a darter or an ibis,
as a lark or a sparrow,
as the great crowned sandgrouse.

FIGURE 6 Migrant man sitting on a CCTV camera outside Melilla, Spain, in Northern Africa. Photograph © by Santi Palacios. Support for the inclusion of Santi Palacios' © photographs in this book was provided by the Class of 1956 Provost's Faculty Development Endowment at Washington and Lee University.

Upon Realizing There Are Ghosts in the Water

Leila Chatti

In memory of the refugees drowned crossing the Mediterranean Sea

I should have known but the water

never told me. It sealed its blue lips

after swallowing you, it licked my ankles

like a dog. I won't lie

and say the ocean begged for forgiveness;

it gleams unchanged in the sun.

Some things are so big they take and take

and remain exactly the same size.

Darkness is like this; grief too. I cry

and the ocean slips from me—all along

a little sea roiling inside with its own

sad phantoms. For a summer I soaked in

its green warmth, wore its salt like gemstones.

Now the heavy shame: how I waded in

to your grave as if trying it on,

how, when the waves came,

they gave me back.

This poem is included in Leila Chatti's book, *Tunsiya/Amrikiya*, Bull City Press, 2018.

Tristeza / Sadness

Marjorie Agosín

En tu mirada moraba la tristeza,
Tristeza color sepia,
Tristeza color ámbar,
Tristeza de las sombras.

Pensaba que en ella, tu mirada, cabía todo el mar.
No era azulada tu tristeza
Como el mar Pacífico que te recibió,
Tampoco gris como el Atlántico.

Era otra:
Era tristeza de la ausencia,
Tristeza de los que no tienen país,
Ni lenguas,
Ni hermanas con quienes salir a pasear.

Regina estaba en los campos de cenizas.
La llamabas ...
Hacías de todos los parques su tumba.

In your gaze dwelt sadness,
Sadness the color of sepia,
Sadness the color of amber,
Sadness of shadows.

I thought your gaze could encompass the ocean.
Your sadness was not the azure
Of the Pacific that welcomed you,
Nor the gray of the Atlantic.

It was another type of sadness:
The sadness of absence,
The sadness of those without a country,
Without tongues,
Without sisters with whom to stroll.

Regina was in the camp of ashes.
You called to her ...
You made every park her tomb.

(Translated from Spanish by Alison Ridley.)

Bienvenus à la jungle de Calais / Welcome to the Jungle of Calais

Domnica Radulescu

THIS PLAY IS INSPIRED by stories of refugees in the camps of Calais, a port in northern France, and it is a companion piece to the play *Crossings* that emerged from interviews with refugees from Mexico, Honduras, and Guatemala. Like *Crossings*, this play is an homage to Maria Irene Fornes' play *Manual for a Desperate Crossing* which was developed from the playwright's interviews with Cuban refugees who traveled from Cuba to Florida in small boats or dinghies. The staging should be both raw, simple, and stylized; like a dream, a hallucinatory atmosphere, avoiding realistic staging.

Characters (in order of speaking parts)

CHORUS: The immigrant characters form a chorus in key moments which, like in Greek tragedy, accentuates the mood or the emotional intensity of the stories, clarifies them or reacts to them and offers moral support. Depending on who is telling their story at any given moment, CHORUS is formed in a spontaneous way by the other characters who are listening. The actors are also spectators. They are telling their own stories, reliving or re-enacting them and at times becoming characters in each other's stories.

VOICE: Menacing loud voiceover that represents the authorities, border police, or the hyperbolic incarnation of the menacing voices of border patrols.

FARID: A seven-year-old Syrian boy who came to Calais with his father.

AMINA: A nine-year old Sudanese girl who crossed the Mediterranean Sea with her mother in a boat.

LULA: Young Eritrean woman who crossed the desert of Libya and the the Mediterranean Sea on her way to Calais.

This play was written entirely at the artists' residency Hôtel de Sainte Valière, France. The author is deeply grateful to the residency, its director and host Eloise Caleo, and to the people of Sainte Valière who warmly welcomed her in September 2019.

ABRISHAM: Young Afghani Woman who escaped to Iran and arrived in Calais.

TESFAY: Young Eritrean man who arrived in Calais after crossing the Mediterranean Sea in a boat.

NASRIN: Young Sudanese woman, mother of AMINA, she came to Calais with her daughter, also having crossed the Mediterranean Sea by boat.

KARAM: Young Syrian man, father of FARID.

Setting

A field of high grass in Calais, next to a woodland, next to a main road, near the entry point in Calais but farther from the port area and the train tracks with the high fences topped with razor wire. The atmosphere of the play is eerie, somewhere between dream and reality.

Time

The present and flashbacks to the past of the characters.

Tableau I

Where do you come from?/D'Où venez-vous?

Two children in the fog in the distance. A boy and a girl appear as if through a fog downstage. They are standing next to each other and looking at the audience. The adult characters are arriving slowly from both sides of the stage as well as from the audience. They stand on each side of the two children at a distance.

CHORUS [CHORUS *here is made of adults, as the two children stand silent and immobile.* CHORUS *moves in the rhythm of the words as if sailing in a boat on wavy seas all throughout the following lines. Their movements as well as words get more and more agitated, louder and faster. At the last words of the chant, "police des frontières" all stop abruptly as if capsized.*]

The waves ...

Les vagues ...

The storms ...

Les tempêtes

The boats …

Les bateaux …

Les barques …

Les bateaux …

Le désert …

The desert …

The Libyan desert

Syria …

The Desert

The Syrian desert

Le désert de Libye

The Syrian desert

Les vagues, les vagues, toujours les vagues …

The waves, the waves, always the waves!

Eritrea …

Syria …

Libya …

Sudan …

The sea and the desert

La mer et le désert

Toujours la mer et le désert

Vagues de sable vagues de mer

Waves of sand waves of water

Les pirates

Ah, oui les pirates

Oohh, the pirates and the sea waves and the sand waves …

Les trains …

Les bateaux …

Trains, ships …

Les camions …

Ah oui, les camions

The trucks and the highways

Les routes, les grandes routes, les petites routes

Roads, highways, large roads, small roads

La frontière …

La police des frontières …

VOICE [*Menacing, loud*] D'où venez-vous? Where are you from?

FARID [*In a steady, monotone voice*] My name is Farid, I am seven years old.

VOICE [*Louder, more menacing*] D'où venez-vous? Where are you from?

AMINA [*The same as the boy, she speaks calmly, in monotone voice*] Je suis Amina et j'ai neuf ans.

VOICE That's not what I asked. Vous êtes bêtes ou quoi?

FARID Quoi?

AMINA Quoi!

CHORUS [*In a mocking way, trying to undermine the authority of* VOICE. *As they do this, all the members of the* CHORUS *get closer to the children and surround them in a protective way*] Quoi, quoi, quoi, pas de quoi, pour quoi, de quoi, je ne sais pas quoi!

[*The two children laugh and look at each other for the first time; they now say their lines to each other instead of to the audience.*]

FARID My name is Farid and I am seven years old. I'm scared.

AMINA Je m'appelle Amina et j'ai neuf ans. J'ai faim. Je n'ai pas peur.

[*In the following lines,* FARID's *and* AMINA's *voices overlap at times, cut each other off, or overlap with a stagger.*]

FARID My name is Farid, I'm scared …

AMINA Je m'appelle Amina, j'ai faim, je n'ai pas peur …

FARID Do you have a piece of bread?

AMINA Tu veux jouer? Je n'ai pas de pain … I'm not scared, I'm hungry.

FARID D'où viens-tu?

AMINA D'où viens-tu?

FARID Je viens de loin …

AMINA Je viens de partout …

[*The other characters are walking slowly around the children and across the stage in circling trajectories as they are also saying their lines, in the same fashion as the children, cutting each other off, staggering their lines with each other.*]

LULA   Je viens du désert rouge ...

ABRISHAM   Je viens de la mer verte ...

TESFAY   I too am coming from the green sea ...

NASRIN   Je viens de la mer rouge de sang ...

KARAM   I too come from the red sea full of blood ...

CHORUS   I come from the red sea

the green sea

the red desert

the yellow sea

the yellow desert

Je viens de la mer rouge

De la mer jaune

De la mer verte

Du désert rouge

From nowhere

From everywhere

Je viens de partout

Je viens de nulle part.

LULA   Et les enfants? D'où viennent-ils? Et où vont-ils?

CHORUS   Aaahh ... les enfants. The children. ... That's different.

Les enfants c'est différent ...

KARAM   On n'aurait pas dû emmener les enfants ...

NASRIN   True, we shouldn't have brought the children ...

ABRISHAM   Yes, that was a mistake, we shouldn't have brought the children ...

LULA   We couldn't leave the children behind ...

TESFAY   You shouldn't have brought the children ...

LULA   C'est vrai ... the children aren't going to make it ... they won't survive the long journey ahead ... And yet, we couldn't leave them behind ...

AMINA   Je viens de la lune ...

FARID   Moi aussi je viens de la lune ...

AMINA   Moi je viens de la lune bleue ... Est-ce que toi aussi tu viens de la lune bleue? Do you come from the blue moon too?

FARID   Ah non, je viens de la lune rouge ...

AMINA   Mon frère est tombé dans l'eau et il est mort. Ma mère est devenue folle.

CHORUS   [*All except for* NASRIN *and* AMINA *take part in this* CHORUS *intervention*] Oh non, quelle horreur, what horror, what horror

Her brother fell in the sea and drowned

His mother lost her mind on the spot

How can she stand it?

How will she survive this grief?

Quelle tristesse de mort

La plus grande tristesse

On peut mourir de cette tristesse

She might die of grief

One can die of such grief

What horror this journey

Ce voyage, on n'arrivera jamais

We'll never make it,

We'll have to make it,

We'll never make it,

C'est pas vrais, on doit réussir

If we have come so far, we have to make it!

FARID   Ma sœur est disparue dans la lune ...

AMINA   Dans la lune bleue ou dans la lune rouge?

FARID   Là ... je ne sais pas. I don't know if my sister disappeared in the red moon or in the blue moon. I only know one day she disappeared ...

AMINA Disappeared, how?

NASRIN Non, absolument pas … on n'aurait pas dû emmener les enfants …

KARAM We should not have brought the children …

LULA We couldn't leave the children behind …

VOICE [*Menacing and terribly loud covering all the other voices*] Silence, silence, silence!

CHORUS [*All characters including the two children cover their ears and scream this time covering* VOICE] You shut up, shut up, shut up, tais-toi, tais-toi, tais-toi!

[*Black out*]

End of Tableau I

Tableau II

J'ai eu un cauchemar / I had a nightmare

[*Eerie bluish lights as if in a dream. All characters are sitting inside or immediately outside a tent. The children are playing a game with buttons and empty tin cans from sardines. The adults are busy at different chores: such as making coats out of black plastic trash bags, cleaning some clothes in a bucket, preparing a meal over a tiny fire in front of the tent.*]

LULA [*She is stirring the meal in the tiny pot with a stick*] J'ai eu un cauchemar … Je marchais dans le désert de Libye, quand mon amie …

AMINA Qu'est-ce qui est arrivé à ton amie?

ABRISHAM [*She is inside the tent, trying to tie together several plastic trash bags into what looks like a raincoat*] Me too, I had a nightmare …, only I was not in the desert like you, I was on the highway … with my brother … when he, when he …

FARID What happened next?

AMINA Oui, oui, raconte-nous ce qui est arrivé à ton frère sur l'autoroute!

FARID Yes, yes, tell us what happened to your friend in the desert of Libya!

KARAM Don't scare the children, no need to recount our nightmares … we have enough of a nightmare right here …

FARID [*Unphased by his father's comments, still curious*] What happened to your friend in the desert? Was the desert hot?

AMINA What happened to your brother on the highway? Were the cars fast?

NASRIN Laisse-les parler, let them talk, ça leur fait du bien, it's good to tell their nightmares. The children must know the truth …

TESFAY The nightmares *are* the truth!

AMINA [*Playfully, as if she is telling a funny story*] Mon petit frère est tombé de la barque pendant la tempête. Voilà, c'est mon histoire!

NASRIN [*She jumps up, grabs* AMINA *and covers her mouth*] Ce n'est pas vrai, it's not true, your brother didn't fall out of the boat, somebody else's brother did, we left your brother home, don't you remember, tais-toi!

AMINA [*Struggling to free herself from her mother's grip, she manages to and goes to the other side of the tent, next to* FARID] Non, maman, ce n'est pas vrai, tu mens, you are lying …

NASRIN [*Starts crying hysterically.* ABRISHAM *and* LULA *hold her and try calming her down.* NASRIN *is shaking and speaking through her sobs*] Ce n'est pas vrai, it's not true, it's TESFAY's brother who fell out of the boat, he fell out and TESFAY tried helping him back up, but the waves were too strong, and he couldn't, his brother tried holding on, but in the end he went down into the waves. You are mixing up the stories, ton frère va très bien, we left your brother with your grandmother … at home, in Sudan …, he is doing very well … il n'est pas tombé dans l'eau, il ne s'est pas noyé parce qu'il n'était même pas avec nous. Tell her Tesfay, isn't it true …?

AMINA [*Stubbornly holding on to her version of the story, crying and talking*] Non maman, j'ai vu mon frère tomber dans l'eau, you wanted to go after him to get him, but the men on the boat didn't let you, they held you and he floated on the waves, then we didn't see him, then you fainted, then …

NASRIN [*Stops crying and becomes catatonic staring in the distance*] On va trouver ton frère, il est là sur la plage, je suis sure. Don't worry my girl, we'll find your brother, he's waiting for us to go get him. He is fine, we'll see him very soon ... I'm so sorry about your brother Tesfay, il n'a pas eu de la chance ... he drowned, maybe it's better, maybe he's happier than we are ...

TESFAY [*As if in a trance, slowly, staring in the distance like* NASRIN] He was raising his arms up in the air, I wanted to jump after him, but they didn't let me, they should have, they should have let me jump ... then he was gone ... nourriture pour les poissons! Food for the fishes! I will never eat fish again, maybe the fish I would be eating has eaten from my brother's body and then I would be eating my brother ...

KARAM Don't you worry Tesfay about that, I don't think any of us here will be eating fish or anything other than these rotten scraps any time soon.

NASRIN Et aussi le frère d'Abrisham ... Don't you know it Amina? Abrisham's brother was also killed, he was run over by a truck on the highway, everybody lost their brother, but we are the lucky ones because you still have a brother ...

ABRISHAM [*Moving towards* NASRIN *in a fury trying to make her stop*] Stop it, shut up, what do you know about my brother and anybody's brother ... just because you couldn't keep your child from falling into the waves ...

NASRIN [*Waking up from her trance, attacks* ABRISHAM, *scratches her face.* LULA, KARAM. TESFAY *get in between them trying to stop them*] My child is alive, the border guards went after him in a big ship, I saw them, they'll bring him to me any minute, they always save the children don't they, they don't let the children drown in the sea, do they? Il est vivant, il est vivant, on l'a sauvé, on sauve toujours les enfants, on ne laisse pas mourir les enfants, vous êtes tous des menteurs! Shame on you for lying about such things ...

[LULA *holds her tightly in her arms until she quiets.*]

CHORUS [*The English and French lines should be said very quickly sometimes one after another, line by line, sometimes the* CHORUS *can be divided in two with one side saying the French the other the English and their lines almost overlapping but not quite.*]

We all lost someone dear	Nous avons tous perdu quelqu'un de très cher
You have your daughter	Il te reste toujours ta fille
You couldn't have done any better	Tu n'aurais pas pu faire mieux
The sea is fierce	La mer est féroce, impitoyable
You survived	Vous avez survécu
With Amina	Amina et toi toutes les deux
The sea spared you two	La mer vous a épargnées
The green sea	La mer verte
The yellow sea	La mer jaune
The red sea	La mer rouge du sang de nos bien-aimés
The red sea full of the blood of our loved ones	
The bodies of our loved ones	Les corps de nos bien aimés
Swallowed by the sea	Avalés par la mer
By the waves	Par les vagues
The red waves	Les vagues rouges
The green waves	Les vagues vertes
The black waves	Les vagues noires

AMINA   Est-ce que les requins vont manger tous les corps? Will the sharks eat all the bodies in the water?

CHORUS   Sshhh Amina, don't ask such questions! Arrête avec tes questions!

LULA   [*She is telling her story while rocking* NASRIN *like a baby*] The desert was beautiful like a yellow sea, we walked for hours, like swimming in a yellow sea, she gave me her last bit of water, I said, I said: no, no, I'm not thirsty, you drink it, and she said, she said: I have more, I swear Lula, I have more water in my backpack … We walked for more hours, I don't know how many, it was getting cold, night fell like a hammer on us, she fell on the yellow sand. I thought she stumbled over a rock, over a small cactus ... I thought just now when we were almost there ... Almost where? Almost where we should be, where we are trying to get, to the people who could help us ... I was talking to myself, trying to give myself courage. She was lying in the sand ... I dug the grave myself, a shallow grave, but a grave nevertheless ... There was no more water in her flask, she had given me her last. I took her backpack ... the village was fifteen minutes away ... Her name is Senait ... it means good luck in Eritrean.

CHORUS   [CHORUS *divide in two groups and chants the English and French lines in a staggered way, so they almost overlap but not completely so the meaning of each can be understood in both languages. The effect must be hallucinatory.*]

You did what you could	Tu as fait ce que tu as pu
You couldn't have done more	Tu n'aurais pas pu mieux faire
You buried your friend	Tu as enterré ton amie toute seule
In the yellow desert	Dans le désert jaune
In the red desert	Dans le désert rouge
In the cold desert	Dans le désert froid

NASRIN   [*Calmer than before, as if waking up from a long sleep*] C'est une très belle histoire Lula, même si un peu triste, merci d'avoir partagé ton cauchemar avec nous. Thank you for sharing your nightmare with us, it's very pretty, even if a bit sad. Don't worry, it's only a dream. Dreams are not true. Your friend will return.

KARAM   We are going tonight! Is everything ready for tonight? Are you ready?

LULA   Are you sure we can all fit in that little thing you call a boat?

KARAM   As sure as I'll ever be Lula, if you don't think so, then you make us another one.

ABRISHAM   Oh, oh, Karam, ne t'en fais pas, don't get mad for nothing, we don't have time for quarrels now. She just asked a question, you know.

NASRIN   Moi je ne vais nulle part, I'm not going anywhere, I've had enough of sea crossings. J'attends Asim, il va venir, I'm sure he'll come soon. He told me in the dream. He said: "maman je suis près de toi, très près, attends-moi."

LULA   [*Whispering to* ABRISHAM] She is delirious again, we have to convince her to get in the boat tomorrow morning, we can't leave her here. On ne peut pas la laisser ici. Elle délire …

ABRISHAM   [*Whispering back*] It's not going to be easy; she won't want to come. You can't convince a mother who just lost a son to do anything she doesn't want to do.

LULA   We have to. Think of Amina, qu'est-ce qu'il va lui arriver si on les laisse ici toutes le deux? Think of something Abrisham, you have your herbs, you know, tu connais les secrets des herbes …

ABRISHAM   Sshhh, ne parles pas de ça, I'll see what I can do.

TESFAY   [*Flustered, coming from the tent*] Notre passeur nous a abandonnés à la dernière minute. We don't have a guide, he pulled out at the last minute. Not enough money, I guess.

KARAM   Qu'est-ce qu'on va faire? On y va tout de meme, we'll go anyways, think of something.

TESFAY   I know the waters better than any of you, I studied the route. We are going no matter what. There are going to be raids this week. I'd rather die in the water than here in this hell hole. I'll take you all no matter what.

NASRIN   Ne parle pas de mourir dans l'eau. Jamais ne parle de ça. Did you hear me, never! Mourir dans l'eau, mourir dans l'eau, dying in the water, what does that even mean? Did anybody die in the water? Do you know anybody who died in the water? Then how come we are all here?

AMINA   Yes, yes Tesfay don't talk about dying in the water, ca fait tellement mal a maman. My mom can't hear you talk like that. Tais-toi!

LULA   Amina, calme-toi, Tesfay only wants to help!

FARID   Yes, Tesfay only wants to help, Amina. Don't be scared, I'll give you my life vest and my collection of buttons, they'll keep you safe, je vais te protéger, I'll take care of you, and when we get to London we'll go inside the big tower together, yes? And you and your mom will be happier, and my dad will marry your mom, and we'll be a family, yes?

AMINA Who said that Farid? Tu parles des bêtises, ma mère ne va pas marier ton père. I don't want your dad to be my dad, I already have a dad, my mother will never marry your dad, you're crazy, leave me alone, laisse-moi tranquille.

KARAM I said we shouldn't have brought the children.

LULA We couldn't leave the children behind.

ABRISHAM It's late, il est tard, il est tres tard, tomorrow we leave at dawn!

CHORUS [*They move in unison as if walking then as if sailing in a boat*] On va partir dès l'aube

We will leave at dawn

On va partir sur les grands chemins

We will leave on the big highways

On the smaller roads

On the sea

Sur la mer

Sur la Manche

On va traverser

We'll cross the Channel

We'll cross in the boat we made

On va traverser dans le canot qu'on a fait

It's only 82 kilometers

We can sail 82 kilometers

If others have done it so can we

On va le faire

D'autres l'ont fait

Nous aussi pouvons le faire.

End of Tableau II

[*Blackout*]

Tableau III

Comment avez-vous traversé La Manche? /
How Did You Cross the Channel?

[*All characters are sleeping inside the tent bunched up together with the two children in between.* KARAM *wakes up first and gently taps everybody to wake up.*]

KARAM   It's time, il est temps, come on!

[*One after the other they wake up from left to right, touching the one next to them and waking them up. It should look like a house of cards that instead of falling it is coming up, quickly but smoothly.*]

TESFAY   Réveille-toi FARID, il est temps!

FARID   Wake up Amina, it's time!

AMINA   Réveille-toi Lula, il est temps!

LULA   Abrisham, wake up, it's time!

ABRISHAM   Nasrin, réveille-toi, il est temps, on y va!

[NASRIN *is not getting up and not moving. We can see her breathing; her body is moving up and down in the rhythm of her breath.*]

LULA   Come on sister, wake up please, we must go. Everything is ready!

NASRIN   [*Speaking softly without getting up*] Allez-vous en sans moi. Je ne viens pas avec vous, j'attends mon fils, il va arriver bientôt. They told me in the dream, they are bringing my son today, the coastguards found him alive and they are bringing him today, I have to wait for him. I am not coming with you.

AMINA   Maman, mon frère est mo …

NASRIN   [*She interrupts her and gets up at the same time*] Yes, it's true Amina, you have to stay with me, we have to both wait for your brother, aren't you happy? Come here, let's wait …

AMINA   Maman, viens, please come! They'll bring him to us when we get to the other side, you'll see!

NASRIN   Non, non, non you are staying with me … Tu restes, tu restes avec ta maman! Amina, reste avec moi!

[*Bright moving lights like a raid are crossing the stage and into the audience a few times. All characters lie on the ground.*]

VOICE   Personne ne part, nobody leaves, all stay! Don't move, you can't pass! Ne bougez pas, don't move! Nobody leaves, personne ne bouge!

[VOICE *goes on and on like a broken record, like a machinery gone wrong. All lie down quietly during the rant. Then* LULA *and* ABRISHAM *whisper something to each other, they go quietly to the end of the tent and return with a tin cup that they hand to* NASRIN *to drink.*]

LULA   If you are going to stay here by yourself, you need strength. Here drink this, it will give you strength to wait until they bring your son to you. Voilà, bois ça, ça va te faire du bien, tu verras!

[NASRIN *drinks the contents of the cup in one long gulp and in a few seconds, she falls back asleep.* KARAM *carries her out of the tent. Everything becomes accelerated after this, the characters put on life vests, then the large cloaks made from black trash bags, they gather all their belongings in other trash bags, pull out the inflatable dinghy from behind the tent and put the tent on fire. We see them carrying the dinghy on their backs and bringing it to the other side of the stage.* KARAM *places sleeping* NASRIN *gently in the boat. They start rowing as if already on water.*]

TESFAY   We all row together. When I say go, we go, nobody stops. If you see coastguards, you raise your hands. Are you ready?

ALL   [*In unison, in rowing position*] Ready, go, on y va!

CHORUS   [*Lines are said in French and English alternatively all throughout the rowing. Images of migrants crossing the English Channel in dinghies and small embarkations should also be projected on stage in the background.*]

We row the dinghy for hours	On rame le canot pendant des heures
In the rough waters	Dans les eaux périlleuses
In the dangerous waves	Dans les vagues dangereuses
It's stormy, it's rough	C'est orageux, c'est dur
The boat almost turns over	La barque se renverse presque

We hold on	On s'y tient
We hold on tight	On s'y accroche
We are close	On est si près
So close	Si près
Almost there	Presque là
A few more meters	Encore quelques mètres
Amina loses a shoe	Amina perd un soulier
Abrisham starts vomiting	Abrisham commence à vomir
Karam is holding Farid	Karam embrasse Farid
It's almost like a long farewell	C'est comme un long adieu
Nasrin is shaking in her sleep	Nasrin tremble dans son sommeil

AMINA   Maman, est-ce qu'on va se noyer comme mon frère?

FARID   You are not going to drown like your brother Amina, relax.

[*The boat is being tossed around by the waves, the waters are violent, the people in the boat are puppets in the hands of the elements.*]

Le Cauchemar de Nasrin / Nasrin's Nightmare

[*Flashback to* NASRIN's *and* AMINA's *previous journey before getting to Calais. A living nightmare.*]

[Voices in a Boat]

Maman les vagues sont si grandes

Are there whales in this sea, mama?

J'ai peur

J'ai froid

Il y a des morts partout dans le bateau

Quel bateau, ceci n'est pas un bateau

Are these people dead mama?

Are there whales in this sea mama?

How about whales?

How about dolphins?

Est-ce qu'il y a des baleines?

Est-ce qu'il y a des dauphins?

Are they dead, are they dead?

Throw them overboard, throw them in the water

Mettons-les dans l'eau, la barque prend de l'eau

The boat is filling with water

Mama why are they throwing the people in the water?

Pourquoi on jette les gens dans la mer maman?

Sont-ils morts, maman, sont-ils morts?

Maman mon ourson est tombé dans l'eau

That's alright, let your teddy go, we'll get another one

Ça va, ça va ton ourson, tu vas en avoir un autre

When we get to, when we get to …

Asim, Asim, Asim, sauvez-le, save him

Il est tombé, il est là, he lost his teddy bear

He wanted to get his teddy bear from the water

Don't let her jump

Let her jump

Stop her

Let her jump, it will make the boat lighter

Maman, don't go

Nasrin calme-toi

Calmez-la

She's shaking the boat

We'll all drown

On va se noyer

Et ensuite?

What happens now?

NASRIN   Amina, as-tu vu ton frère, il était là il y a une minute.

AMINA   Non, maman, mon frère est tomb…

NASRIN   Ah, of course you didn't see your brother, we left him with your grandmother, we left him home, bien sûr que tu n'as pas vu ton frère, c'est parce qu'on l'a laissé chez sa grand-mère. Maybe there was a war, oui il y avait une guerre, sans doute il y avait une guerre, but even with the war, your brother is safer at his grandmother's house ... he has food and toys there ... it was better with the war, la guerre était meilleure ...

Are we there yet, mama, are we there yet?

Where, where are we?

Il fait si noir, it's so dark,

Maman j'ai peur

Maman j'ai faim

Maman j'ai soif

L'ourson flotte sur la mer

N'aie pas peur ma petite,

On est là, on est arrivé

Ton frère arrivera bientôt

Bientôt

Bientôt

On va manger bientôt

On va dormir bientôt

My brother's teddy bear is floating on the water!

Maman, voilà l'ourson de mon frère,

It's not your brother's teddy bear

It's someone else's teddy bear,

D'autres enfants se sont noyés ici

Mais pas ton frère

Not your brother

On arrivera bientôt!

Tout va venir bientôt, tout, tout

Tout est bientôt

We're here

On est là, là, là.

Où est on arrive?

On appelle cet endroit la jungle

This is called the jungle

It's the jungle of Calais

We made it, what do we do now

That we made it to the jungle of Calais?

We wait and rot in the camp

Drowning in the sea would have been better!

Oui, maintenant on pourrit dans les camps

C'était pour rien,

On aurait dû se noyer dans la mer!

Don't say that, don't ever say that!

Ne dis pas ça, jamais ne dis ça!

Parfois la mort est meilleure!

Sometimes death is better!

C'est pas sûr, on ne saura jamais

We'll never know, but you are here!

Mais vous êtes là!

[*Nightmare ends and we are back in the boat that is crossing the Channel and being tossed in the waves.*]

LULA   I can see a boat, a ship, we are close aren't we Tesfay?

KARAM   Yes, very close, hold on well, tenez-vous bien, very very close, we'll get there soon.

TESFAY   We'll get there soon brother, but the sea is rough. Rougher than we thought. La mer est dure, plus dure qu'on avait pensé!

ABRISHAM   We should throw our bags in the water, it will make the boat lighter. On est trop lourds, la barque est trop petite … on a trop de choses … too many things …

AMINA   Maman, ne jette pas notre collection de boutons, ça nous apporte de la chance. Don't throw our button collection, it brings us luck. Throw the food, elle est pourrie et mouillée.

FARID   Yes, throw away the food, it's all rotten.

LULA   Don't throw away the water. Jamais l'eau, gardez l'eau.

FARID   We don't need the water, look, water everywhere!

AMINA   It's not good for drinking dummy, don't you know that? It's seawater, on ne peut pas boire l'eau de la mer, l'eau de la mer ça ne se boit pas, on en meurt, you die if you drink this water!

LULA   Keep the water, gardez l'eau. Keep the water!

Le Cauchemar de Lula / Lula's Nightmare

[Flashback to LULA*'s crossing the desert of Libya with her friend.* LULA *speaks like in a dream, and she plays all the characters/voices in her story.]*

Le village est là …

Le village est loin, très loin,

Non, le village est tout près, il est là

No, it's far away, the village is far

I'm telling you it's close

How much water?

A little bit, there is still some water left

We'll get there soon

The water, the village, the sand

L'eau, le village, le sable

We'll get there before dark

The village is close, very close

We'll get there before dark.

My flask is empty

Ma bouteille est vide

On va arriver à la mer bientôt

Non, c'est la mer de sable

Non c'est la mer de la mer, de la vraie mer, je te dis mon amie

There is no sea nearby, only the sand sea, only sand waves

You misunderstood my dear, there is no sea, a water sea,

Only sand seas, waves of sand

The oasis, the village with the oasis is nearby

Drink the water, there is more, I have more Lula

There is plenty of water in my flask, trust me

La nuit tombe, il fait froid, c'est bien, j'aime le froid

Lève-toi, lève-toi, lève-toi, le village est là!

Please get up, you're just tired, the village is close!

A sandstorm, on ne voit rien

The heat, I can't see a thing

The cold, I can't see a thing

The cold sand under my hands,

This hole is too shallow, it's too cold

It's only a shallow grave, a cold shallow grave

It's only a makeshift grave

You can't have a real grave in the desert

It's just for now, we'll come later with people from the village

We'll give you a proper burial later

The village is near, le village est là

Your bottle is empty, you lied to me,

I drank the last drop

Why did you let me drink the last drop of water?

In the morning when it's not too hot not too cold

I'll come back with water and water your grave

Le village est là!

J'arrive au village, il n'y a personne

Qu'est-ce que je fais maintenant que je suis dans le village?

Raconte-nous ton histoire dit quelqu'un

Quelle histoire, je n'ai pas d'histoire.

Si, si tu as une histoire, avec ton amie dans le désert.

The camp counselor asks me to tell her my story

She insists I tell her my story,

I have no story I say,

What story are you talking about?

When I got to the village at night

And my friend was dead and buried

The village was dark, everybody must have died there too

Or they didn't want to talk to foreigners

I never went back to rebury her.

Yes, yes, I understand but tell us your story

She kept saying, we need to hear your story

I have no story, je n'ai pas d'histoire,

I should have been dead, it should have been me

She would have made a deeper grave for me

And she would have returned to water my grave

Je n'ai pas d'histoire, j'aurais dû être morte

Je suis plus morte que vivant, je dis à la conseillère.

Non, tu es plus vivant que morte

En effet tu es vivant, tu es là,

I am more dead than alive I tell the counselor in the camp

Leave me alone I say, I am more dead than alive

She says, she says: you are wrong, you are much more alive than dead,

In fact, you are alive, you are here.

[*The flashback has ended, and we are back on the sea in the boat.*]

TESFAY   We are almost there, hold on tight, keep rowing! One more
wave and we're in British waters, I see the coastguard post.
When I say row, we all row, one, two …

[*At three a huge wave raises the boat then tosses it around, then washes over
them. The boat reemerges.* TESFAY *is in the water, all others are
still in the boat.*]

Le Cauchemar de Tesfay / Tesfay's Nightmare

Une seule seconde, c'était rapide

It was all so fast

No, I'm wrong, it took forever

Ça a pris longtemps, des années et des siècles

Une mère pleure je ne sais pas pourquoi

I have no idea why this mother is crying

Il y a toujours une mère qui pleure quelque part

Dans une barque, dans un bateau

Dans une flottille, on s'en faut le nom de l'embarcation

There is always a mother crying somewhere

In a boat, ship, dinghy, who cares what you call it

My brother says we'll get there soon Tesfay,

Je vois Calais, regarde au loin, tu vois, tu vois?

Je dis, je dis je ne vois rien, il n'y a que l'eau partout

Ne te penche pas, ne te penche pas, ne te penche pas je te dis

Je ne me penche pas, je regarde

Don't lean over I say, we are not on vacation,

I'm not leaning over brother, I'm just looking

Quand on arrive je vais dormir pendant vingt-quatre heures

J'appelle maman et je lui dis maman on est là, à Calais

On l'appelle la jungle, mais ce n'est pas si mal que ça

I call my mom and I tell her mom, I say, mother we are here

We arrived in the jungle, that's what they call this place in Calais

But it's not so bad,

C'est un endroit comme tous les autres, avec beaucoup de gens comme
        nous qui attendent

Et ce n'est pas la guerre.

It's just like any other place, and there is no war.

Je ne sais plus rien, je ne me souviens plus

Je dis à la conseillère que je ne me souviens plus

De comment mon frère est tombé dans l'eau,

I tell the camp counselor that I have no idea,

I don't remember how my brother fell over,

Ce n'est pas important, il s'est penché un peu

Il avait hâte d'arriver

Il y avait une grande tempête,

Cependant la mer était calme

Le ciel était orageux, mais la mer calme

Ou le ciel était calme et la mer orageuse

He leaned over and there was a storm, the sea was wild

Or no, maybe the sea was calm, but the winds were too strong.

Les conseillers veulent toujours connaître les détails

Pour qu'ils se sentent bien, qu'ils ont fait leur boulot.

The counselors always want to know the details

So they feel good about having done their job.

C'est pas la faute à la conseillère que ton frère et toi vous êtes partis sur
       la mer, 60 personnes dans une petite merde de flottille de dix
       personnes,

Elle veut seulement aider, c'est ce qu'on dit.

It's not the counselor's fault that you and your brother left

In a shitty dinghy that was meant to carry ten people and you were sixty in
       all, that's what some people in the camp told me.

Ce qui m'obsède surtout c'est qu'il a dû penser : il va sauter me sauver, mon
       frère va me sauver et puis qu'est-ce qu'il a dû penser?

Puisque je ne suis pas allé le sauver?

C'est ça, qui m'obsède.

Qui parle, qui raconte et qui est raconté?

L'histoire n'est pas importante

La mer mange tout.

What really gets to me is that he must have thought I was going to jump
       and save him

What did he think in the few seconds before he died?

Who is telling this story? I tell the counselor I don't know.

Who is telling this story? I have no idea why my brother fell in the water but
       he did.

All I know is that the sea swallows everything.

[*The flashback has ended; we are back in the dinghy on water,* TESFAY *is still
       fighting the waves trying to survive.*]

    KARAM   Hold on brother, keep swimming, the coastguards will get
          you.

      ALL   [*Raising their hands and shouting*] Au secours, Help, help us,
          man in the water! Aidez-nous!

NASRIN   [*She has woken up and is resigned to having been put on board despite her will*] I'm coming to get you mon fils, don't give up, je viens, je viens, don't be scared, you'll make it, je viens mon enfant …

[*She jumps in the water after* TESFAY.]

AMINA   *Maman, non!* Come back, please mommy come back! Reviens, reviens, mon frère t'attend de l'autre côté, my brother is waiting for us on the other side, I'm sure they got him, didn't you say we were waiting for him mommy?

VOICE   [*This time* VOICE *is that of a British coastguard noticing the embarkation with migrants. Though it is loud and harsh, it is not hostile and forbidding like the one in the previous scenes*] Stop! Who is there? Attention, attention all posts, small embarkation with people, two people in the water, all posts. Stop! I said stop!

[*Two coastguards jump in the water to save* TESFAY *and* NASRIN. *A larger coast-guard boat comes over to the dinghy and helps the remaining people on board. They get* NASRIN *but* TESFAY *is taken by the waves.*]

KARAM   Tesfay won't have to worry about eating fish that ate his brother any longer. He is at peace now.

LULA   We owe him our lives; without him we couldn't have done it!

FARID   Is he dead? Papa, did Tesfay die?

ABRISHAM   He went on a journey, he'll be back, I'm sure … he'll be back … people like him don't die … easily …

[*All are now in the coastguard boat.* NASRIN *is being resuscitated by one of the crew.*]

LULA   He was so close, we were so close, we were so close to making it together, all of us!

NASRIN   [*She is coming to and understands the entire situation. She has a new clarity and calm*] On a sauvé les enfants, we saved the children, au moins les enfants sont saufs … I did my best, sometimes one's best is not enough. Tesfay, pauvre Tesfay!

[*The six people are brought to shore. Empty stage, all actors are standing in line downstage as if ready to be interviewed.*]

VOICE   Nom, prénom, nationalité! Name, surname, nationality! Nom, prénom, nationalité, name surname, nationality!

[*Loud news bits about refugees crossing the Channel or found dead on the shores of the Mediterranean, electoral campaign, etc. Images of migrants crossing the Channel, living in the tents of Calais, or of bodies on the beaches of the Mediterranean should also be projected.*]

Brutal border policies at Calais ... increasingly dangerous crossings to Britain ... French authorities said they found 30 migrant including 11 children trying to cross the English Channel ... la photo d'un petit Syrien âgé de trois ans ... mort noyé dans le naufrage ... the photo of a three-year-old Syrian boy ... dead ... dead, drowned on the beach ... près de 17,000 morts sont disparus en Méditerranée depuis 2014 ... morts sur la plage, noyés ... dead on the beach ... noyés ... morts ... dead, ... on the beach, sur la plage ... seventeen thousand died or disappeared trying to cross the Mediterranean since 2014 ... Tunisian beaches ... more corpses than tourists ... little boy drowned on the beach ... refugee crisis ... in Calais the refugees suffer from many health problems due to lack of proper facilities and hygiene ... refugees are not offered emergency shelter from the French government or any other countries ... la campagne électorale de Marie Le Pen ... protéger la France ... protect our country ... close the borders ... close the borders ... protect our country, la France aux français.

[*One by one the actors come close to the audience speak directly to them as if they were reporting to the public, in a detached manner, or as if the audience were the interrogators.*]

AMINA   Je m'appelle AMINA, j'ai neuf ans. Je viens de loin. My name means trustworthy. Je suis triste pour Tesfay. My mother almost drowned like my brother because she wanted to save Tesfay. I'm happy my mother was saved.

FARID   I am Farid. I am seven years old. I come from everywhere, mostly from the sea. My name means unique. I'm happy we left Calais, it stunk there. My dad is very brave, he helped everybody and built our boat, sometimes I miss my mom, I don't know where she is, maybe she was lost in the sea too like the others. Une nuit je faisais dodo dans un camion et quelqu'un m'a réveillé très fort, I thought it was my dad, but it was the police.

NASRIN   Je m'appelle Nasrin, je ne suis plus jeune … je ne sais plus d'où je viens, I have no idea where I come from … possibly from the dead.

KARAM   My name is Karam, it means generous in Arabic. I'm not sure I'm so generous, it's all about survival. Tesfay didn't make it in the crossing, and I feel responsible, he guided us on the sea and he should have made it, he was so close. But the others made it. The children made it, c'est bien.

ABRISHAM   Je m'appelle Abrisham, ça veut dire "soie," it means silk. Je viens de la guerre. On the way to Calais we were 30, only four of us survived, me and my brother and two others. Then my brother was killed by a truck on the highway. Qu'est-ce que je vais faire en Angleterre? I don't know! My name means silk, I have no idea why, je n'ai aucune idée pourquoi on m'a appelée comme ça.

LULA   Crossing the sea is worse than the desert. My name is Lula, it means warrior. I'm glad my friend died in the desert and not in the sea, at least I could bury her. She was so close to the village. Like Tesfay to the rescue boat. They almost made it but then they didn't. At least we saved the children.

VOICE   [Loud and jarring, goes on like a broken record] Nom, prénom, nationalité, name, surname, nationality, reason for leaving your country, nom, prénom, nationalité, raison de quitter votre pays, name, surname, nationality, reason for leaving your country …

[Blackout]

END OF PLAY

Refugee Song

Mihaela Moscaliuc

Sixteen lost at sea survived
at her breast.

When her mind tangled in sea grass,
lips kept the milk flowing:

dying women, men, ghostling of newborn
afloat among damselfish.

The shore pushed them back
toward lands poisoned by war.

Father, all you ever did
was gorge on my flesh.

My belly grew eyes
but the pelvis shrank,

thinned by vinegar
and grazing nails.

What am I to call
your hunger,

the teeth marks
clotted with milk,

the shore I barely reached?

This poem first appeared in *Immigrant Model*, University of Pittsburgh Press, 2015.

Boat

Khaled Al-Maqtari

This is a Yemeni refugee girl who lives in the Yemeni refugee camp in Abakh, Djibouti. As women and children go out for a walk, they walk about three kilometers away from the camp to the shore. There, they see a boat pulled up on the beach. The boat tells them stories of immigration. The boat is a tool for the exploration of countries, freedom, and dignity. The children run like seagulls on the beach, and there are many questions in their minds. "Are there any countries that can provide us that which we lack?" A girl named Anfal and her friends climb into the boat. There Anfal's eyes well up with tears about her past and the fear of the unknown. She jumps into the boat to sit down and rest, tired from the miles of travel, from playing, and from her thoughts.

The Refugee Considers the Faucet

Philip Metres

After Pamela Argentieri's "Continued Persistence"

O arm that spurts flowers,
Branch giving birth to water.
O tree that bows down

And stays there, hovering
Between sky and ground.
You anchor us to now.

We have walked so long
Our home has narrowed
To the width of our shoes

And what we can carry.
And yet you, still animal,
Hollow metal

Conducting an internal
Convo with movement,
You are endurance

In the still moment
Of beginning, you are
Anticipatory beauty,

O instantaneous river,
Compressed creek,
O brass wellspring,

Invisible lake, O slake,
Oasis in a tube, taproot,
Song of the mute, I bow

To you, and hold my hands
Like a shallow bowl
Beneath your mouth.

This poem first appeared in *Paris Review*, issue 228, Spring 2019.

Yemeni Fisherman

Khaled Al-Maqtari

It is hard to brave the sea. But it is impossible to do so only with traditional means.

This is a picture of a Yemeni refugee whose name is Fares Abdullah Awad and who lives in a central camp for Yemeni refugees in Abakh, Djibouti. Behind this fisherman there is a child no more than twelve years old. The child's name is David. David and his father catch fish in a very traditional way. The boat is made simply, out of the remnants of plastic boxes. Its outer shell is covered in plastic materials rescued from the remains of the refugee's home. The photograph transmits a sense of challenge and hope. The challenge comes from the refugee's superhuman ability to overcome the difficulties he faced in surviving. Hunger compelled him to be creative. He braved the sea on a giant boat, which is difficult, but he did it with very traditional methods. This sounds impossible. Finally, hope exists as long as his love for life remains.

Scydra · Carabia · Gallicum · Ossa · Argilus

Arnissa · Cithum · Lete · Anthemus · Bolbe · Posidium

Pella · MYGDONIA · Auton · Bromiscus

Corrites Lake · Extrant R. · Pella · BOTTIÆA · Sindus · Therme or Thessalonica · Moryllus · Boll · sa · jurus · Capros I.

Ichnæ · Lydias R. · Chalastra · Cissus · Duodea · Heraclea · Aspinia · Chalcdca · Calarna

KORDÆA · Bocra · Ascorus R. · Alorus · Hegonium Pr · Gigonus · Chabrias R. · Augea · P. Pan · P. Panomus

Bermius M. · Galadra · Methone · Æneium Pr. · Eneia · Smila · CHALCIDICE · Antigonea · Olynthus · Pilorus · Sin

MEA · Agassæ · PIERIA · Pydna · Æneum Pr. · Thermaic · Combrea · Lipaxus · Spartolus · Olynthus · SITHONIA

Phylace · Balla · Pytna · Petra · Methone · Potidæa or Cassandria · Torone · Cophos · Canastr

Ēane · Mieza R. · Dium · Ega · Aphytis · PALLENE · Mende · Posidium Pr. · Canastr

Libethra · Heracleum · Phila · Peneus R. · Posidium Pr.

Imbunii M. · Æane · Enipeus R. · Eurymnæ · Mendae

Asorius M. · Oloosson · Pythium · M. Charax · Myræ · Homolium · Tempe

Doliche · Pharsalus R. · Dodone · Gonnus · Elatia · Elone · Gyrton · Nesonis L.

Oxynia · Cyretiæ · Atrax · Phalanna · Sycurium · AE · G

Melibœa · Mallœa · Mule · Phricium · PELASGIOTIS · Larissa · Mopsium · Dotium · Rhizus

omphi · Pieria · Metropolis · Phacium · Phacium · Cranon · Melambium · Amyrus · Melibœa

Ithome · Tricca · Pelinna · Pharcadon · Cynoscephalæ · Ossa M. · MAGNESIA

Peneus R. · THESSALIA · Pherae · Glaphyra · Iolcos · Casthanæa

Stimo · Lampsus · Pharsalus · Palepharsus · Theudium · Thyllus · Demetrias · Pagasæ · Ormenium · Sepias

Achorne · Proerna · Narthacium · Thebæ · Demetrium · Spalatra · Olizon · Sciathos · Scope

Theama · Cypara · Phalacthia · Thaumaci · PHTHIOTIS · Alos · Phylace · Tisaeus M. · Scopelos

Calathana · Metropolis · Melitæa · Hellas · Ptelcum · Dium · Peparethus · Peuce

Sosthenis · Cimene · Xynias L. · Phylace · Histiæa or Oreus · Artemisium

Angæa · DOLOPIA · Xynia · Larissa Cremaste · Telethrius M.

Homila · M. Othrys · Acyphas · Lamia · Phalara · Echinus · Canæ Pr. · Cerinthus

Sperchix · Macra Come · Anticyra · Maliac G. · Thermopylae · Cnemides · Gulf of · Ædepsus · Phalasia

R. Sperchius · Hypata · Trachis · Nicæa · Scarphea · Alope · Cynus · Opuntius · Egæ

ÆNIANES · Heraclea · Cnemides · Atalanta I. · Anthedon

DORIS · M. Œta · LOCRIS · Opus · Dirphossu M.

Boium · Charadra · Amphicæa · Elatia · Hals · Larymna · Corsea · Anchoe · Orobiæ

Cytinium · Lilæa · Tithorea · Cephissus R. · Hyampolis · Cortonius M. · Cyrtone · Anthedon

Ŏchalia · Amphissa · Parnassus M. · Lycorea · Abæ · Psoos M. · Dalganeus · Chalcis

Tricha · Ægitium · Myonia · Delphi · Daulis · Orchomenus · Holmones · Copa · Aulis

Corax · Chaleron · Crissa · Cyparissus · Panopeus · Cheronea · Lebadea · Acræphia · Schœnus · Mycalessus · Delium

Apollonia · Hyæa · Curha · Pleistus R. · Triodos · Ambryssus · coronea · Copais Lake · Hyliaca L. · Teumessus · Tanagra

Calydon · Potidania · Tolophon · Anticyra · Medeon · Stiris · Haliartus · Ascra · Thespiæ · Thebæ · Asopus R.

Erythræ · Oeanthe · Apoll. Pharstii · Marathus · M. Helicon · Leuctra · Parnes · Decelea

Naupactus · Bulis · Thisbe · Plataea · Eleutheræ · Phyle

Patræ · Ægium · Cerynea · Corinthian Gulf · Pharygium Pr. · Siphæ · Cithaeron M. · Œnoe · Thria

P. Mychus · P. Eubtrus · Creusa · Pegæ · Ægog

Thermaic Gulf · MAGNESIA · Pagasæan Gulf

Okay When Are We Going

Leila Chatti

> "They're not coming to this country if I'm president. And if Obama has brought some to this country they are leaving, they're going, they're gone."
> Presidential candidate Donald Trump on Muslims entering the USA

My mother says to us, over pasta, *Okay, when are we going*
to talk about the elephant in the room? We're at a restaurant,
me and my sister and our Arab father wedged between our white
boyfriends and, at the far end, our brothers who've darkened
like berries with time. At first we don't know
what she means, butter knife gripped in her fist like a spear,
but then she spits it out, voice lowered, as if it's obscene—
Trump—and all of us swallow, even if our mouths are empty.
What I knew, before, of the word was little—something
to do with wielding a winning hand in a game
I was unprepared to play. And I suppose I've always felt
that way: placed just outside a circle I was desperate
and hoping to join. My father, when he came to this country,
carried with him his passport, his god, and a handful
of words like coins. My mother taught him her tongue, which I understood
as love. And understood, too, when, that summer after the towers sank
like a heart, she pinned the tiny striated flag to my breast
before my flight back *there*, the other land, as though it might protect me
from this one. My mother, looking the same
as she does now, white-lipped and terrified, in a Midwestern restaurant
ten days 'til Christmas, snow fluttering past the window
like flakes of ash. That summer, back where she could not reach us,
they lined us up like stars—splayed us with toes and fingers touching,
my brothers six and five. I was a child. I cried. The flag shuddered on my chest.

This poem first appeared in Leila Chatti's book, *Tunsiya/Amrikiya*, Bull City Press, 2018.

Where Do I Go?

Eric Garcia

"Where Do I Go?" is part of a politically charged series of cartoons entitled
El Machete Illustrated, by Eric Garcia (copyright).

A Strange(r's) Dress

Jennifer Schneider

Damascus, Syria—March 2011

My sisters always admired my style.
"Which should I choose, Laila?"
the six of them would ask.
Despite my younger self, I served
as the trusted voice of fashion
for our close-knit sisterhood.
Hours spent selecting perfect fabrics and fasteners.
Delicate silks, sturdy cottons, smooth pearled buttons.
My basket of supplies manufacturing
the magic that is someone's favorite dress.

Home, Damascus—April 2011

Carving out minutes to craft my own forever favorite.
By hand. I refer to her as "The One".
Secretly, of course.
The dress that knows me as well as
I know every thread that is its soul.

My Workshop/Damascus—June 2011

A final needle, pulled tight. Seamed and knotted.
My dress. Perfect.
A spirited collage of shades of red and orange.
Crimson, crushed mandarin, burnt copper, carrot, and ruby.
Golden threads mixed with silver gauze.
A tapestry of lush woven satin and silk.
Soft, brushed cotton on the underside
A palette reflecting a full life. Sassy and fiery.
How we lived and breathed. Daily.

Celebration/Market Days, Damascus—July 2011

First wear. First outing.
Slim fitted bodice. Elastic at the waist.
A flared ruffle at the skirt's edge,
catching soft breezes of air.
Sprinklings of glitter. Everywhere.
Practical but pretty, I liked to say.
Hidden under the back collar and the tiny privacy clasp.
A cream tag with my initials – L.F.M.
Letters threaded with gold speckled yarn.
A tiny, incandescent star in the top right corner.
Papa's nickname for me. His light.

Dozens of blackberry hives decorated the long, full skirt.
Tiny flowers embroidered across the bodice.
Tulips of pale blue, yellow, and pink petals.
Shimmer in natural light.
Deep green stems and lush leaves.
Reach towards the sun. The stars.

A small stain decorates the left sleeve.
Noticeable only to me and my daughter. Sweet Mala.
A way to remember our outing, we said.
Tiny drips of melted cheese,
forms five petals. Darker in the middle.
Like a plumeria flower,
mirrors our ten intertwined fingers.
Eternal Spring, we laughed.
Until the darkness came. Always.

United States—March 2016

Spring.
At home during the months of March through May,
but warm year-round.
Forced to flee. To unknown lands.
Not expecting to land a butterfly,
but hoping to emerge as such from a later cocoon.

New Hampshire, U.S.—April 2016

Now here, northern New Hampshire,
A land of mountains, highway, and strange accents.
Rooms full of waist-high furniture, with nowhere to pray.
Somewhere between home and the unknown.
Climates change, so do people.
Each season, and myself, more bitter and cold.

North Conway, N.H.—May 2016

Some 5,456 miles from home. Syria.
My dress and my memories worn from travel and war.
The once vibrant fabric, now dirty with soot and tears.
My sisters left behind. Mama and Papa, too.
Foreign mud,
caked under previously cherished fibers.
Frayed threads. More each day.
Back buttons, sequins,
falling one by one.

New Hampshire—June 2016

Longing to belong. Somewhere.
Losing a forever home. Still seeking another.
Not here. No longer there.
Nowhere.

Manchester, N.H.—July 2016

Images of my people on the newspaper's front pages.
The Times. The Daily's. The local magazines.
I study them. Searching for my kin.
Seeing us in body, but not in soul.
Black and white photos,
strip our color.
Ourselves.

N.H./New York/N.H.—August 2016

Fearful of speaking. I button my lips.
Unsure of the language. I zipper my mouth.
Afraid to offend. I patch my eye.

Fresh Settlements, New York—September 2016

I brought the dress with me that first Spring.
An always favorite, that now feels too short.
Even as it grazes the falling leaves around my feet.
The fabric hangs loosely across my frame.
Once a beloved ornament,
emerges as a marker of my otherness.

New Seasons/New Beginnings, New York—October 2016

Fleece hoodies. Piles of lettered tees.
Cartoon ducks, cats, and Superheroes.
Corduroys and velvets in new cuts.
Denim jackets. Woolen sweaters.
Markers of my otherness.
Washed and pressed. Presented as gifts.
Made for another's frame. A different life.
Earlier worn by strangers. Scented with kindness.
Infused with a casualness I do not understand.

Thanksgiving/N.Y.—November 2016

I packed it away. The One.
Folded carefully. A solemn good-bye.
Right arm pulled over,
placed at 90 degrees. Left arm following suit.
Crossed. Bottom up. Corners tucked.
A perfect square. No longer perfect.
Checked loose threads. Knotted them tightly on the underside.
Like my stomach. Hiding signs of wear.
Cardboard box. Lid on top.
Fearful it, and I, will never fit again.

A Map of Migration Routes

Philip Metres

Each line is arrowed red.
Inside, they tumble

across muscled continents
like erythrocytes, millions

of flesh-tucked skulls hauling
the heaviness of dreams. Red for departure,

blue for return. Their lives
shrunk to a single cell

they palm to their chest
in bus depots and windowless tents

at night, seeking a signal,
a recognizable voice, someone

home, lithium ions draining.
When they sleep, they sleep

in clots of human waking.
When given paper and crayons,

their children draw weapons.
Red for departure, blue

for return. Like veins, the lines
draw back to the heart, the heart

where the rivers flooded,
or the fields baked in drought,

where the guns came out,
having traveled from somewhere far,

and guns made love to guns,
making more guns,

and the blood began to run.

This poem first appeared in *The Rumpus*, December 20, 2018.

Refugee Snow

Matthew Murrey

Not shovels,
not the dread skid
to the ditch,
not even salt, no,
just childish rejoice
for what's free,
falling and frozen,
yet floats like luck's feathers—
long flight from bad
to better, hunger
to dinner, cot to bed
and comforter.
It's contagious
this spontaneous
jump, jump, run and twirl,
this smiles up to taste
and palms out to catch
the sky falling:
fluffed tatters of icy white
that turn, on touching
skin, to a blessing of water.

This poem first appeared in *Poets Reading the News*, November 17, 2018.

Home Is Where They Let You Live

Jasmin Darznik

"WHERE IS YOUR HOME?" the consular officer asked me.

I was thirteen years old. My parents and I had left Iran eight years earlier, at the onset of the 1979 revolution. Since then, they had bought a house and a business—a small roadside motel in California. I had gone to school and learned to speak English. Then, on a summer trip to visit my mother's Iranian relatives in Germany, I made the mistake of calling America my home.

The trouble started when my mother handed me the visa forms. My father had stayed behind to run the motel, and even though my mother had learned enough English to get by, at moments like this, when it was just the two of us, I was still the translator and all-purpose intermediary between "us" and "them." I took the clipboard and began filling in the papers. My parents and I were in the United States legally, but since we'd traveled outside the country, my mother's business visa would need to be renewed. It was standard procedure—we wouldn't have encountered any difficulties if, under the line asking where our home was, I hadn't written "America."

"Are you sure about that?" the officer asked me, her pen pointed at my adolescent cursive. When I nodded, she retreated to a back room. A few minutes later, she returned to inform us that our applications had been denied. We would not be able to return to America, because we had expressed an intention to stay in the country permanently.

Looking back, the certainty of my response astonishes me. The Iranian revolution and the vagaries of immigration law had dispersed my relatives all over the world. By the time I faced that consular officer, I had cousins in Wisconsin, Stockholm, Istanbul and all points in between. During our time in Germany, my mother stayed up long into the night, reminiscing with my aunts and uncles about Iran and speculating about the country's future—and the possibility of returning there someday.

But by that time, I had spent several years distancing myself from the country then known as "Eyeran." I had seen enough footage of the

This essay first appeared in the Opinion section of the *New York Times*, May 26, 2012.

hostage crisis. I had been called a "smelly A-rab" at school, watched my mother get stared down in grocery shops on account of her accent and witnessed the sharp looks my veiled grandmother drew in the streets. I had quickly learned not to be Iranian in ways that showed. I plucked my eyebrows, bleached my hair with Sun-In and hitched up my skirts. My accent was pure Valley girl, heavy on the "likes." By summer's end, I was desperate to get back to California. A visa was the only thing standing between me and the only country I cared to claim.

The first thing I noticed at the American Consulate, where we went to fill out the necessary forms, was the line of people snaking around the building. Most were dark-skinned, and more than a few of the women were veiled. "Refugees," my uncle explained. "They come every day in hopes of getting visas." His voice trailed off, making it perfectly clear how they fared.

Because my father had German citizenship, I had a German passport, too, and that meant my mother and I were permitted to skip the line and enter by a different door. That door, and its false promise of entry, would soon become very familiar to me. And with each trip we made to the consulate and each denied petition, the distance between us and the refugees grew smaller, and the possibility of returning to America more distant.

* * *

Over the next several months, the mattress on my cousin's bedroom floor became my bed. I learned to speak Persian fluently again because it was the only language my family and I shared. Back in America, my father ran the motel, saved money for a lawyer, and devoted himself to filing appeals for us. He persuaded the local high school to let me take my classes through correspondence work. My German wasn't good enough to enroll in a local school without intensive remediation anyway, and what was the point if we'd soon be leaving? Eventually, my mother rented us a basement apartment, but strictly on a month-to-month lease. "We'll be back in a few weeks, you'll see," she explained.

When I wrote to my American friends, I never explained why I hadn't returned at the end of the summer. I made it seem like a choice, like we were having such a wonderful time that we'd decided to extend our vacation. They mailed me letters and mix tapes, and I hoped they wouldn't forget me. But despite my mother's reassurances, the truth was that I started to think I might never return to America.

As it happens, I did return, nearly two years later. After several unsuccessful attempts at filing appeals for us on his own, my father was finally able to hire an attorney. Six months after that, my mother and I were free to come back, though with the explicit promise that we'd be staying only temporarily and only for business reasons.

Of course, so much had changed by the time I returned. The first—and in some ways most enduring—shock came at the airport in San Francisco, when I couldn't recognize my father in the crowd. Two years of running the motel on his own and wrangling with immigration bureaucracy had left their mark. He'd gained a lot of weight, and wrinkles fanned out at the corners of his eyes. He was also much sadder than I remembered, but then I'd left as a child and returned much more grown up, and I could see him differently now.

America, though not wholly strange, was no longer familiar to me. Before, I'd willed myself into looking and sounding as if I belonged. Though I could still pass as American, I now had the sensation of perpetually looking at everything from the outside. Home schooling, paired with exile, had made me more shy and introspective, if also more independent. I was a real immigrant now.

Each year many thousands of children are brought to America by their parents. They come before they have any concept of citizenship, much less of belonging. Like me, they will draw their notions of "home" not only from what is familiar and desirable but also from what is permitted and denied them.

Today, I am a permanent resident. I can go and come easily, but at borders I am still reduced to the girl who once made the mistake of calling America her home. I check and recheck my passport for my green card. It's always there, right where I put it, along with the uncertainty, the fear and, yes, the anger I'll never quite outrun.

"Home." At 13, I had that notion knocked out of me in ways that were useful, or mostly so. But the word still makes me uneasy, and even now, whenever I am given a choice, I leave the answer blank.

Refugee

Kenneth Hada

A little girl sleeps on the ground.
Her mother's worry is her worry now.
Her hunger is her mother's hunger.

Her brother and father are ghosts
remembered before the ground
swallows her tears un-swabbed.

A voice throbs within: Home—
Where? Not Here. Somewhere.
Does she understand her fate

she who embodies the hate of others,
brings Republicans frothing
into weird, cowardly alliance

with indifferent churchgoers who,
once again, mis-pledge their allegiance?

This poem first appeared in Ken Hada's collection *Not Quite Pilgrims*, VAC Poetry, 2019.

Alien Resident

Mihaela Moscaliuc

My mother rescues bitter cherries off Queens Boulevard.

She catches and hoists them in the net of her pleated skirt,

cradles them to her employer's kitchenette.

On a leather barstool that spins into night, she pits and pits,

keeps pace with the vermicular fanfare, bitter blood

under nails, petite castanets cackling in the dry mouth.

On the trenches of dawn, crushed flesh dissolves in the sugar bath

as she nods, on one elbow, to the squeals of bedroom doors.

She spoons coffee, keeping count aloud, and pours milk for kids' pancakes

as instructed, with a measuring cup. The perfect scale of her eyes

she wastes on homespun sanitizers—⅔ vinegar ⅓ peroxide—

for sinks, counters, her Eager Beaver, his dumbbells.

She jogs through the day in bark slippers, elm

embossed with perfectly knifed hearts.

What's she doing here, my mother, in a toddler cot,

apron pockets lined with shriveled fruit worms, jars of preserve

ticking under the mattress like hand grenades.

This poem first appeared in *Immigrant Model*, University of Pittsburgh Press, 2015.

In the Promised Land

Mihaela Moscaliuc

Each border-crosser bleeds.
On parole from the American dream,
I daymare through new famine outbreaks,
through history's torture chambers
refurbished by self-fashioned demagogues
aroused by their own voices and unleashed cruelty.

Each border-crosser bleeds.
The air clots with a familiar miasma,
an intimate abnormalcy
signposted with flags and boots.
No foot should rest on a head,
though I'm not the one to speak.

I adored my grandfather. He named me Diana,
took me to the tyrant's sequestered forest
to forage for mushrooms
and rule over snowdrops and forget-me-nots,
charged me with plucking pellets
out of skinned rabbits. Each border-crosser bleeds.

I was so hungry when I landed.
For years my throat tickled with *yes please,
some of each*: sizzling fajita, drenched ribs,
seared ahi on bales of seaweed, banana split,
an invisible warden always ready to sprint
if I did not lick my plate clean.

Proactive, I lined pantry shelves
with enough Campbell's cans to last
another dictatorship and pasted pantry doors
with photographs that plotted history' variables.
In one, six foresters, my grandfather among them,
smile gloriously, arms locked shoulder to shoulder

in a human chain. My grandfather's foot
rests on a bear's head. *This one's honey
had been laced with sleeping pills. We had
to make sure Ceaușescu brought it down on first try.
He might have disappeared us otherwise.
Who knows.* Who knows.

Ban Jesus

Eric Garcia

"Ban Jesus" is part of a politically charged series of cartoons entitled El Machete Illustrated, by Eric Garcia (copyright).

J'y suis j'y reste /
Here I Am, Here I Stay

Cristina A. Bejan

Characters

THE IMMIGRANT: (he/his)—must have an Eastern European accent.

THE CHORUS: three actors (male, female or non-binary), playing all other characters (friends, family, etc.)—actors must use appropriate accents (CNN American, American Southern, Eastern European, and Ethiopian) depending on the character.

Setting

Suggested that a member of the cast introduce each scene, stating the setting. There is a backdrop screen that could display each setting; on this screen the subtitles should be displayed translating the Romanian and French into English; this is also an opportunity to display photographs, first in black & white then in color, of THE IMMIGRANT's life (as well as other images and video) at the discretion of the set and projection designers. Settings include a courthouse and specific locations in Galați, Romania, Cambridge, MA (USA), and Durham, NC (USA).

Music

This play is about the exile finding home in music; hence the essential dimension of music throughout the play. Song suggestions are strongly advised.

Scene 1: Galați, Romania

[THE IMMIGRANT *is playing a basketball shoot-around with his friends, Adriano Celentano's "Ciao Ragazzi Ciao" is playing in the background during the dialogue.*]

FRIEND #1: America, ragazzo! (America, our friend!)

FRIEND #2: Ne laşi pentru totdeauna. (Leaving us forever.)

THE IMMIGRANT: Nu, voi ştiti ca o să mă întorc. (No, you guys know I'll be back.)

FRIEND #2: E doar chestiune de timp. (Just a question of when.)

FRIEND #1: Cred că din cauza bursa, trebuie să te întorci? (I guess with the scholarship, you have to come back right?)

THE IMMIGRANT: Da. Desigur. (Yes. Of course.)

FRIEND #1: Asta nu conteaza de loc, tu ştii. Ajungi în America, rămâi aici, prietene. (That doesn't matter at all, you know. You get to America, you stay, man.)

THE IMMIGRANT: Aşa zice şi mama mea. Dar o să fie foarte greu pentru ei aici. (That's what my mom says. But it will be hell for them here.)

FRIEND #2: [*under his breath*] Securitatea. (The Secret Police.)

FRIEND #1: Serios frate, uită-ne pe noi acum. Poţi sa joci baschet în Boston! (Seriously bro, forget us for now. You can play basketball in Boston!)

THE IMMIGRANT: Mă întorc inapoi, serios. Nici engleza nu o vorbesc incă. (I'm coming back guys, for real. I don't even speak English yet.)

FRIEND #1: Sunt sigur ca mulţi oameni nu vorbesc engleza în SUA. Este o ţară plină de imigranţi. (I bet a lot of people in USA don't speak English. Immigrant country.)

FRIEND #2: Poate limba franceză şi rusă o să-ţi fie de ajutor. Poate întâlneşti o doamnă din Rusia acolo. (Maybe your French and Russian will come in handy? Meet a nice Russian lady there?)

THE IMMIGRANT: Tatăl meu ar avea un atac de cord. (My dad would have a heart attack.)

FRIEND #1: Prietene tu mergi în America! Primul din Galaţi! O să-ne fie dor de tine. (Dude, you are going to America! The first of Galaţi! We're going to miss you.)

FRIEND #2: Hei, înainte de a pleca, hai sa vedem o ultimă aruncare liberă cu mana stînga. (Hey, before you leave us—let's see if you make one last left-handed free throw.)

FRIEND #1: [*giving* THE IMMIGRANT *a high-five*] Ai primit-o. (You got this.)

[THE IMMIGRANT *goes up for a shot with his left hand. Lights down on his follow-through.*]

Scene 2: MIT Basketball Team Tryouts

[*Nancy Sinatra's "These Boots Are Made for Walkin'" playing quietly in the background.*]

MIT BASKETBALL COACH: You've got good form and a nice jumpshot. You're on the team.

THE IMMIGRANT: [*very nervous with poor English*] Thank you coach.

MIT BASKETBALL COACH: You'll need to get some shoes–legit basketball trainers.

THE IMMIGRANT: [*clearly not understanding*] Shoes? I'm sorry … .

MIT BASKETBALL COACH: Yes, go buy your own sneakers just like everyone else. [*Turns his attention back to tryouts.*]

CHORUS MEMBER: With that, THE IMMIGRANT walked out of the basketball tryouts and out of the gym. He never played basketball ever again. He was too embarrassed to tell the coach why and honestly at that stage he didn't speak enough English to maybe ask for help. THE IMMIGRANT—like so many before him and since—came to America with $60 dollars in his pocket (his parents' life savings). And in Romania, the basketball team provided you with everything: your shoes, uniform, bag, etc. This experience made THE IMMIGRANT decide two things: the first, he didn't need to play sports in college, he needed a job; and second, he was going to one day be a great scientist. The next day he started work as the janitor of the Mechanical Engineering Department at MIT.

Scene 3: The First Good Will Hunting

[*The backdrop of this scene is Jefferson Airplane's "Somebody to Love."* THE IMMIGRANT *is performing many janitorial tasks and keeps running into the* AMERICAN LADY. *He is wearing a lab coat that is fraying at the edges only held together with binder clips and rolling large canisters of liquid nitrogen in the department's basement while the* CHAIR *of the Mechanical Engineering Department is giving the new secretary, the* AMERICAN LADY,* *a tour of the building—no words are exchanged with* THE IMMIGRANT. *He is mopping the floor, and the* AMERICAN LADY *walks by with some papers. He's replacing rolls of toilet paper in each bathroom. The* AMERICAN LADY *walks out of the women's room, as he is going into the men's. And finally he enters the* AMERICAN LADY's *office and empties her trash. After exiting her office and disposing of her trash, he returns with a question.*]

THE IMMIGRANT: Hi, could I please borrow a pencil?

AMERICAN LADY: Yes, of course. [*She hands him a pencil.*]

THE IMMIGRANT: Nice to meet you.

AMERICAN LADY: [*very confused*] Yes, nice to meet you!

THE IMMIGRANT: Are you going to the departmental dinner?

AMERICAN LADY: I am!

THE IMMIGRANT: So am I.

AMERICAN LADY: Ok?

THE IMMIGRANT: [*decisive*] So we go together.

AMERICAN LADY: Sure? [THE IMMIGRANT *nods his head and backs out of her office.*]

THE IMMIGRANT: Thank you for the pencil. [*Then he runs off. Jefferson Airplane continues to play.*]

CHORUS MEMBER: It was during these early years that American rock music enveloped THE IMMIGRANT and provided the comfort he needed as he missed his family. As his degrees went by—first Bachelor of Science, then Master's, then PhD—it became clear that he would not return to Romania. His most prized possession from this time was a photo in his MIT yearbook of him at a campus Grateful Dead concert, before they became the Dead we know today. His face is peaking out in the back behind the band while Jerry Garcia plays in the center of the tiny stage on a campus lawn somewhere. Hippies! THE IMMIGRANT and the AMERICAN LADY had a pretty rocking love affair during this time and married. This meant he could technically stay in the States but it wasn't so simple. It never is.

[*Lights fade as Grateful Dead's song "Truckin'" plays.*]

Scene 4: Letter from Romania

[THE IMMIGRANT *is seated, reading a letter from his mother. She is seated writing the letter on the other end of the stage. She reads these words in Romanian as she writes. The English is projected on the screen. We see* THE IMMIGRANT*'s reactions while she reads. By the end he is weeping.*]

THE IMMIGRANT'S MOTHER: Ne este dor de tine. Galațiul este pustiu fără tine. Tatăl tau se simte din ce in ce mai rău. În cele din urmă, l-a luat hepatita. În fiecare seară am grijă de el. Cred că sfîrșitul este aproape. Supravegherea devine din ce în ce mai severă, așa cum știam că va fi deoarece tu ești în stăinătate. Noi suntem părinții unui dezertor. Sunt urmărită în fiecare dimineață în drum spre farmacie și în drum spre casă. Sunt convinsă că ne ascultă prin pereți. Telefonul nostru este cu siguranță ascultat. Tatăl tău nu vrea să spună nimic acum. A construit un pat tocmai deasupra ușii din față. Serios. Oricum doarme toată ziua. Dar el stă pe acest pat acum, pentru că atunci când Securitatea va veni în mod neașteptat, așa cum o fac în mod constant, nu o să-și dea seama că e cineva înăuntru. El spune că ei pleacă din moment ce ei nu văd pe nimeni atunci când intră în apartament. Există altceva despre care nici măcar nu vreau să-ți spun ca să nu-ți faci griji. Dar m-a consumat într-un mod în care nu mi-aș fi imaginat niciodată. Fratele tău și-a pierdut mințile. Pur și simplu nu-și poate controla gândurile. Consumul de alcool i-a scapat de sub control, acest lucru ți-l amintești. E ca și cum un demon a pus stăpânire pe el. Polițiștii l-au luat de pe stradă și l-au băgat într-un azil lângă Iași, un azil de nebuni. Nici măcar nu-mi pot imagina condițiile și pacienții de acolo. Mă doare inima cînd mă gândesc ce a văzut el acolo. M-am dus imediat acolo să-i cer eliberarea. Doctorii de acolo l-au pus pe Haloperidol, le-am spus că sunt farmacistă și pot să am grijă de el. După două săptămâni de insistențe, ei au fost de accord. Fratele tău a fost eliberat și noi am avem grijă de el aici. El pare ca se simte mai bine, luîndu-și medicamentele. Nu sunt sigură ce să spun, ce să cred. Și eu am suferit mult de gânduri dificile, dar să văd în el, atîta rău. Ce înseamnă asta pentru familia noastră? Este clar că trebuie să trăim cu acest blestem. Mă rog, fiule, ca această nenorocire să nu ți se întâmple ție și familiei pe care o construiești în America.

(We miss you here. Galați feels empty. Your father is getting worse and worse. The hepatitis is finally taking him. Every night I spend caring for him. I see the end coming very soon. The surveillance is getting more severe, as we knew it would with you continuing to be out of the country. We—the parents of the defector. I am followed every morning on my way to the pharmacy and on the way home. I am convinced they are listening to us through the walls. Our phone is definitely tapped. Your father refuses to say anything now. He built a bed—believe this—over the front door. He is sleeping all day anyway. But he stays on this bed now, so that when the Securitate burst in unexpectedly as they constantly do, he is hidden from them. He says they just leave now, since they don't see anyone when they enter the apartment. There is something else—I don't even want to tell you—to worry you. But it has consumed me in a way I never could have imagined. Your brother lost his mind. He simply lost control of his thoughts. His drinking was out of control, this you remember. But it is like a demon took him over. The police picked him up off the street and put him in an asylum outside of Iaşi, yes, an insane asylum. I cannot even imagine the conditions inside and the other patients. It hurts my heart to think what he saw. I immediately went there to petition his release. The doctors there put him on Haloperidol. I told them, I am a pharmacist, I can take care of him. After two weeks of begging them, they relented. Your brother was released and we have been taking care of him here. He seems better taking this medication. I am not sure what to say. What to think. I have suffered difficult thoughts myself but to see it in him, so much worse. What does this mean for our family? We clearly carry this curse. I pray, son, that this affliction will never happen to you and the family you are building in America.)

[*This scene closes with Gianna Nannini's "Io senza te."*]

Scene 5: From the Convenience Store to the Apartment Building

[THE IMMIGRANT *is walking from the convenience store to his and the* AMERI-CAN LADY'*s apartment in Cambridge, MA. He is being followed by a US-based Securitate* AGENT, *who is wearing a black trench coat and smoking a cigarette.* THE IMMIGRANT *looks back a couple of times, clearly aware that he is being followed. Once he reaches his building, he sharply turns around and confronts the Securitate* AGENT *in Romanian.*]

THE IMMIGRANT: Îți dai seama că suntem în Statele Unite ale Americii? (You do realize that we are in the United States of America?)

AGENT: Da, desigur. (Yes, of course.)

THE IMMIGRANT: Nu-mi poți face rău aici. Ceea ce faci tu este ilegal. (You can't harm me here. What you are doing is illegal.)

AGENT: Ilegal? Tu esti ilegal. Ai încălcat legea română stând aici. (Illegal? *You* are illegal. You have broken Romanian law by staying here.)

THE IMMIGRANT: Sunt căsătorit cu un cetătean American. Prin urmare, sunt aici legal. (I am married to an American. Therefore I am here legally.)

AGENT: Îți vom găsi o soție mai bună în România. Tot ce trebuie să faci e să te întorci. (We will find you a better wife in Romania. All you have to do is return.)

[THE IMMIGRANT *turns away and starts to open the front door of his apartment building.*]

AGENT: Știi ce ești cu adevărat. (You know what you really are.)

THE IMMIGRANT: [*turning back*] Ce sunt, domnule Securist? (And what's that, you Securist?)

AGENT: Ești doar un dezertor. Un trădător. Un inamic al statului. (You are just a defector. A traitor. An enemy of the state.)

THE IMMIGRANT: De fapt, sunt om de știință și soț. (Actually I am a scientist and a husband.)

[THE IMMIGRANT *slams the door behind him. The Doors' "Break on Through" starts to blare over the loudspeaker.*]

Scene 6: The Courtroom

[*Immigration court.* THE IMMIGRANT *and the* AMERICAN LADY *are there, accompanied by their lawyer. They are standing in front of the* JUDGE.]

JUDGE: You, sir [*referring to* THE IMMIGRANT], when did you come to the United States?

THE IMMIGRANT: 1969.

JUDGE: I know you have been in immigration courts for almost ten years now, so you have heard all these questions before. But I have to ask, I am sure you understand.

THE IMMIGRANT: Yes, of course, Judge.

JUDGE: How did you come from Romania? I understand it is a strict regime, also our enemy in the Cold War.

THE IMMIGRANT: A government scholarship, sir.

JUDGE: Seems odd that they would offer scholarships to America. In return for what? What was the catch?

THE IMMIGRANT: [*very reluctant*] Everyone who received it—well, it happened at Otopeni airport—right before we were getting on the plane to leave.

JUDGE: What happened?

THE IMMIGRANT: We were forced to sign a document.

JUDGE: [*pressing*] What kind of document?

THE IMMIGRANT: A document saying we were members of the Communist Party, sir.

LAWYER: But you have to understand, Judge, they were forced to do this. This was not voluntary. In order to study in the States this was the *quid pro quo.*

JUDGE: Oh, I understand perfectly. [*Addressing* THE IMMIGRANT.] As you are no doubt well aware, this is no longer the McCarthy Era. But we are engaged in the Cold War. Some would argue that we are at the height of this conflict. You know all this, I am sure. The US does not accept communists to become naturalized US citizens. In fact, we don't really want anyone from the Eastern Bloc to stay here, it's dangerous. You know, from an intelligence perspective, I am sure you understand.

THE IMMIGRANT: Of course I do, sir.

JUDGE: [*turning to the* LAWYER] Here's the deal, you prove without a shadow of a doubt that this man is not a communist. Then you have a case. I understand he is married to an American but because of this "communist" label, it's not enough, I am sorry.

LAWYER: [*to* THE IMMIGRANT *and the* AMERICAN LADY] We can do this, I promise.

AMERICAN LADY: [*hugging* THE IMMIGRANT] I love you.

THE IMMIGRANT: I love you too.

[*"Everything's Alright" from the original* JESUS CHRIST SUPERSTAR *album begins to play and continues until the end of Scene 6.*]

CHORUS MEMBER: [*pause*] Fast forward, their lawyer kept his promise. THE IMMIGRANT was granted US citizenship and sworn in at the courthouse in Denver, Colorado when his wife was six months pregnant with their first daughter. How did they get there from Cambridge? Well there was a really long post-doc in California and then—finally– THE IMMIGRANT landed his first real job at CU-Boulder. Two years there and another daughter born, the four moved to Perth, Australia for his first sabbatical. Then to Durham, North Carolina for good. Duke University had found out about this guy. He was hired with tenure and four years later became the youngest chaired professor in the university's history. You would think that by this point, THE IMMIGRANT would consider himself a great scientist. But he was just getting started.

Scene 7: The Center of their House in North Carolina

[*The* AMERICAN LADY *and* THE IMMIGRANT *are directing their daughters to pack big cardboard boxes in the center of their house.*]

#2 DAUGHTER: [*pointing inside one of the boxes*] T-shirts. Soap. Cigarettes.

#1 DAUGHTER: Who will get these packages, Dad?

[THE IMMIGRANT *is holding an orange envelope and one by one pulls out a black & white photograph, each photo is projected on the screen.*]

THE IMMIGRANT: Your cousin Mirela. Your uncle Virgil and his wife Liviana. My cousin Camelia. Your grandmother.

#1 DAUGHTER: Grandma from Romania!

THE IMMIGRANT: Yes, my mother.

Scene 8: The Daughters' Bedroom

[THE IMMIGRANT *is tucking his daughters in at night. They have twin beds. He sits between them.*]

THE IMMIGRANT: What story tonight girls?

#1 DAUGHTER: Nuşu and the stuffed owl from the basketball trip!

#2 DAUGHTER: Your uncle's head in the pumpkin!

#1 DAUGHTER: Throwing rocks in the streets—wish we could do that here.

#2 DAUGHTER: I want to hear about the poop in the river.

#1 DAUGHTER: Castrating Seeky the cat by stuffing its head in the boot! Or maybe your parents' love story? I always love that one.

THE IMMIGRANT: As you know, they were students, attending university in Bucharest. First in their families to go to college! Your grandfather Anghel was on a military scholarship.

#1 DAUGHTER: He protected the horses in the war.

THE IMMIGRANT: Yes he did! He was a doctor! He took care of all animals.

#1 DAUGHTER: That is how he knew how to cut Seeky's balls off.

THE IMMIGRANT: A veterinarian. So he and my mother were at a military ball in a big building in the middle of Bucharest called the Military Circle. They danced and they kept dancing all over the city. They fell in love. Romania was free then, girls.

#2 DAUGHTER: Free like America?

THE IMMIGRANT: Yes, we were a democracy.

#1 DAUGHTER: So what happened? Why did communism come?

THE IMMIGRANT: It was fascism first actually—like the Nazis in Germany. Then communism. After World War II the American and British leaders gave Romania to Russia—the Soviet Union—so the country became communist—that's why I left.

#1 DAUGHTER: That's not fair! Romania was a democracy like our country. I don't understand.

#2 DAUGHTER: Do you miss your family Dad?

THE IMMIGRANT: Yes, yes, I do.

Scene 9: Driving around Durham in the 1980s

[THE IMMIGRANT *and his daughters are in his car. Sade's "Sweetest Taboo" plays.*]

#2 DAUGHTER: Who is this Dad?

THE IMMIGRANT: Sade.

#1 DAUGHTER: Sade is from Nigeria!

THE IMMIGRANT: So girls, where in Africa is Nigeria?

#1 DAUGHTER: West Africa!

THE IMMIGRANT: Right. See, there's a reason we have a globe next to our dinner table.

#1 DAUGHTER: [*totally moving on*] Can we listen to Paula Abdul?

#2 DAUGHTER: Yes! After Paula Abdul, can we listen to Michael Jackson?

#1 DAUGHTER: Yes! After Michael Jackson, can we listen to Fine Young Cannibals?

THE IMMIGRANT: Cannibals?

#1 DAUGHTER: Dad! You know them. Mom took us to their concert, remember?

THE IMMIGRANT: Ok girls, hand me the box of cassettes and let your dad be your DJ.

[*The girls hand their dad a shoebox of cassettes from the backseat.*]

DAUGHTERS: Yay!

THE IMMIGRANT: One day you will like Sade, you will see.

#1 DAUGHTER: I'm not saying I don't like her! I just really look like Paula Abdul.

[THE IMMIGRANT's *eyes widen slightly terrified. The daughters can't see. He switches out the Sade cassette for Paula Abdul's* FOREVER YOUR GIRL *album—"Straight Up" begins to play.*]

Scene 10: Their Kitchen

[THE IMMIGRANT *is on the phone frantically speaking in Romanian to his best friend Vali in Bucharest. His* DAUGHTERS *are running back and forth from being with the* AMERICAN LADY *watching the TV blaring with news from Romania and checking on their dad in the kitchen.*]

THE IMMIGRANT: Nu primim destule știri aici, Vali. Doar violența de pe străzi și Ceaușescu evadând cu un elicopter. Tu, Anca și Anamaria sunteți în siguranță? Ce să însemne asta? Vom fi liberi ca restul Europei? (We are not getting enough news here, Vali. Just the violence on the streets and Ceaușescu flying away in a helicopter. Are you, Anca and Anamaria safe? What does this mean? Will we be free like the rest of Europe?)

[*There's a pause as* THE IMMIGRANT *listens to Vali's reply. Then* THE IMMIGRANT *stops abruptly and drops the phone to the floor.*]

THE IMMIGRANT: [*crying, tears falling down his face*] Ceaușescu is dead!

DAUGHTERS: Dad!!!!

[THE IMMIGRANT *sweeps up his* DAUGHTERS *in his arms and dances around the kitchen as Queen's "I Want to Break Free" plays.*]

#1 DAUGHTER: What does this mean?

AMERICAN LADY: [*emerging delicately from the TV room with a two-month old baby in her arms*] It means your dad can go back to Romania, girls.

#2 DAUGHTER: Can we go too?

AMERICAN LADY: Yes, we all will go.

[DAUGHTER #2 *jumps out of her dad's arms and runs to hug her mom's legs.* DAUGHTER #1 *and* THE IMMIGRANT *dance as "I Want to Break Free" plays. Lights down on a family embrace.*]

Scene 11: Ride to School

[THE IMMIGRANT *drives up to the school. Car is blaring Eros Ramazzotti's "Cose Della Vita."*]

THE IMMIGRANT: [*as his* DAUGHTERS *are opening the side door to the minivan*] Get good grades!

DAUGHTERS: Yes, Dad, we know!

[*The* DAUGHTERS *run off to school.* THE IMMIGRANT *pulls away.*]

Scene 12: Homework Time

[*Later that night, back at home. Alanis Morissette's "You Learn" plays softly.*]

THE IMMIGRANT: Girls! You know what time it is?

#1 DAUGHTER: Ugh, Dad.

#2 DAUGHTER: Do we have to?

THE IMMIGRANT: You'll thank me eventually.

[THE IMMIGRANT *pulls out a Romanian math textbook.*]

THE IMMIGRANT: Let's do pages 10 and 11 tonight.

#1 DAUGHTER: Algebra?

THE IMMIGRANT: Romanian students learn algebra at your age.

#2 DAUGHTER: But we don't even know Romanian!

THE IMMIGRANT: Math is the universal language. You can read math.

[*The scene ends with* THE IMMIGRANT *passing out notebooks and pencils and his* DAUGHTERS *dutifully tackling the problem sets.*]

Scene 13: The Mean Streets of Durham, NC

#2 DAUGHTER: So our dad may have driven us to school every morning but you think he drove to work from there? You gotta be kidding me. He drove back to our house and left the car for my mom to use. Then he would walk to work. Yes, from our neighborhood Forest Hills to the university! He had this golf ball that he would bounce his whole walk—he said it helped him think. So he walked miles and miles—I don't know how many—lasted an hour I think—to get there. And the same exact path back. He walked through neighborhoods that had nothing in common—most people would think it most dangerous his daily routine. He had this friend who lived on the corner of one of the windy intersections—this was a much older man, Southern, a very thick accent, had served in the military. I remember my dad taking us to this man's birthday party one year. Everyone there was so Southern. We were curious about this invitation—"Who is this guy, Dad?" "Girls, I talk to him every day. He is my friend." And that was that. When my dad's friend died, I could tell that my dad was going through something. But typical, you know, he didn't talk about it. Maybe this was how it was for him his whole life? First Romania, then Durham. Friends always falling off the map. For a man and a culture that really needs friends, this must have been hard. But he always had his science right? He always had his work right? The thing I find most notable about these walks is that my dad became a local celebrity. Durham didn't—doesn't—have sidewalks. Everyone at school would say, "So, that's your dad?" Yes, my dad was the only human being walking around Durham. And he was useful. Before GPS, how did people find their way around? They stopped their cars, rolled down their windows and asked my dad. His adopted city became a map in his brain. My sister calls it: "Spatial memory." He walked until his back couldn't take it anymore, so for something crazy like 20 years. Now he swims, whoa, and that's another story.

[*Mylène Farmer's "Dessine-moi un mouton" has started playing and plays into the next scene.* #2 DAUGHTER *exits.*]

Scene 14: Bojangles'

[THE IMMIGRANT *driving in his car with his two daughters. They pass a sign on the highway for* BOJANGLES', *the Southern fast food restaurant.*]

DAUGHTERS: Bojangles'!!!! Please?!!!

THE IMMIGRANT: It's not the one we normally stop at but that's ok—let's do this girls!

[*He turns off the highway and into the Bojangles' lot. The three walk in and up to the counter. Soul for Real's "Candy Rain" plays over the restaurant's sound system.*]

THE IMMIGRANT: We getting the usual?

#1 DAUGHTER: Yes, obviously, Dad—a big box with chicken and biscuits!

#2 DAUGHTER: And iced tea.

THE IMMIGRANT: [*to the* BOJANGLES' EMPLOYEE] Hello! We'd like your box with 14 pieces of chicken with four biscuits and three unsweet iced teas.

BOJANGLES' EMPLOYEE: [*in a very Southern accent, stopping in her tracks*] Sir. Sir, are you from England??

THE IMMIGRANT: Excuse me?

BOJANGLES' EMPLOYEE: You sound like you are from England!

THE IMMIGRANT: No … no … .

#1 DAUGHTER: [*laughing*] It's your accent Dad! [*to the Bojangles' employee*] My dad is from Romania.

THE IMMIGRANT: [*almost correcting her*] I am from Europe.

#1 DAUGHTER: He thinks he is from Italy and France.

THE IMMIGRANT: Europe, see?

BOJANGLES' EMPLOYEE: [*laughing*] Amazing! I have never met anyone from there! So you said the Supreme box and three unsweet teas.

THE IMMIGRANT: No ice for me please.

[*He pays with cash and carefully counted exact coins. He needs no change.*]

BOJANGLES' EMPLOYEE: There are you are. You know anyone ever tell you, you look just like James Bond?

[THE IMMIGRANT *blushes and smiles broadly.*]

#1 DAUGHTER: All the time, don't flatter him!

#2 DAUGHTER: But we only have one mom—in case you were wondering.

THE IMMIGRANT: [*proudly*] Yes, my wife! Let's go girls—get the food—

BOJANGLES' EMPLOYEE: Y'all have a good one!

[THE IMMIGRANT *and his* DAUGHTERS *pick up their food and go sit down to eat their meal together. Not in the car on the go like Americans do.*]

Scene 15: Each night stays up till 2am working from the beginning till end

[*Takagi & Ketra's "L'esercito del selfie" ft. Lorenzo Fragola, Arisa, plays on repeat throughout this scene.* THE IMMIGRANT *is sitting at his work desk, alternating between working on his computer and writing/drawing by hand on paper. The time is projected on the screen. Starts off at 8pm, just after dinner. We see the time pass to midnight, then to 2am. At which point,* THE IMMIGRANT *closes his laptop and the music cuts out. He steps up and walks downstairs to the bedroom.*]

Scene 16: The Immigrant's Piazza #1— Southsquare Mall

[*Boyz II Men's "Motownphilly" plays in the background.*]

CHORUS MEMBER: For decades THE IMMIGRANT's piazza was Southsquare Mall in south-central Durham, about a ten-minute drive from his house, which he calls "the White House." He took his family of five there every Saturday to eat one large cheese pizza from Sbarro, always ordered extra crispy. Every Saturday as his daughters would hang out in various stores and meet up with friends, he would first talk to the owner of Sbarro for a minimum of 30 minutes, just to catch up on the week. Then he would make his rounds throughout the Food Court, greeting every small business owner and manager and seeing how they were doing. The Korean woman who owned Dairy Queen to the Latino man who managed McDonalds. He checked on everyone. Once he would return to his family and the pizza he would take his two slices and scrape the cheese off. His daughters *loved* that part—the extra cheese was theirs! He put all the pizza seasonings you can think of on top and ate his crispy crunchy bread. "Would you like a piece of bread?" That's THE IMMIGRANT's famous line! Then something happened that upset THE IMMIGRANT's exiled balance. A developer bought Southsquare. The Mall was demolished. Cosco and Target moved in. His Saturday trips ended abruptly. This coincided with his children going off to college (the best colleges obviously, I mean they are half-Romanian and did get good grades!) and then graduate and law school. His little carefully crafted European society in the Brooklyn of the South collapsed in on itself. So what did THE

IMMIGRANT do? He found another piazza … but this one? He goes to every single day. At 4pm exactly.

Scene 17: The Immigrant's Piazza #2—Harris Teeter

[*In Durham's first Harris Teeter, located just behind where Southsquare used to be. Céline Dion's "My Heart Will Go On" from the movie* Titanic *is playing over the grocery store sound system.* THE IMMIGRANT *is making his rounds through the store—it is clear that he is acting like clockwork. He stops by the fruit, chooses some bananas. Next stop the bakery: he selects his baguette. Now at the fish, he asks the* HARRIS TEETER EMPLOYEE *for the usual. Next up the red wine, of course. After investigating several, he selects a bottle from South Africa. He swings by the refrigerators in the back and picks up his orange juice. Now time to check out, he heads to the front of the store and puts all of his five items on a checkout belt. Another* HARRIS TEETER EMPLOYEE *checks him out, while* AHMED, THE IMMIGRANT'*s friend from Ethiopia, starts to bag his groceries. Once* THE IMMIGRANT *finishes paying, they bag the rest together.*]

AHMED: Hey man, good to see you!

THE IMMIGRANT: Wait—when was the last time Ahmed?

AHMED: Yesterday!

[*They laugh in ridiculous unison.*]

THE IMMIGRANT: Congratulations Ahmed! Just saw that your prime minister won the Nobel.

AHMED: That and the news says we're the most welcoming country in the world. But you know me, happier to be here man, happier to be here.

THE IMMIGRANT: Don't get me started Ahmed! Have you heard this rumor that the American Dream is not possible? That's what's out there now—that's what I hear.

AHMED: Tell them to go back then. Leave America for us.

THE IMMIGRANT: Right on! Hey, the Arsenal game this Saturday, you gonna watch it?

AHMED: Of course man! The only thing I'll get up at 5am for.

THE IMMIGRANT: Me too, me too. I feel like we are not where we should be in the League.

AHMED: It's Manchester. I'm telling you. We just got to keep fighting.

[*They have packed up the cart and* THE IMMIGRANT *is good to go.*]

AHMED: I'll see you man!

THE IMMIGRANT: Yes thanks Ahmed, see you tomorrow.

[THE IMMIGRANT *waves goodbye to his friend and pushes his grocery cart towards his car.*]

Scene 18: The American Dream?

[THE IMMIGRANT *sits in the driver's seat of his car. Next to him sits a* CHORUS MEMBER. THE IMMIGRANT *reaches back for his shoebox of CDs and flips through them during this conversation. He settles on one by Algerian-French group* ZEBDA *and puts it in the CD player.*]

CHORUS MEMBER: So where is THE IMMIGRANT going now in Durham, North Carolina in 2020? You're 72 now, right?

THE IMMIGRANT: Yes I am! First to my office, then Harris Teeter, then back to the White House, make dinner, work till 2am, sleep, repeat.

CHORUS MEMBER: Seems like you are here to stay.

THE IMMIGRANT: Where would I go now? I am home. As one very wise man of Algerian origin once sang in this great song [*motions to the CD player*]: J'y suis j'y reste.

CHORUS MEMBER: Is that Algerian?

THE IMMIGRANT: [*shaking his head at American ignorance and laughing*] It's French, you kill me! Algerian is not a language!

CHORUS MEMBER: [*embarrassed*] Sorry?

THE IMMIGRANT: Yes, Americans don't know languages … or history … or geography … or math.

CHORUS MEMBER: So what does the song title mean?

THE IMMIGRANT: Thank you for asking. I listen to this one in secret—no one knows but you now.

CHORUS MEMBER: Wow—this is an honor!

THE IMMIGRANT: Yes. It means: "Here I am. Here I stay." [*Pause.*] You know, the YouTube video is banned in America. [*Laughs.*] Those Zebda guys really shook things up!

[THE IMMIGRANT *turns his car on, presses play on the CD player and backs out of the driveway. He drives to his office with his music playing and* CHORUS MEMBER *grooving to the North African beats. English subtitles of the song displayed. Lights down only after the first chorus of "J'y suis j'y reste" 4×. The song continues for the curtain call and as the house opens for patrons to leave.*]

END OF PLAY

Swallows Sing the Night to Sleep at Lansing Station

D.A. Lockhart

Here, they disembarked
from points strewn
across a double line
of metal hammered
into wood and laid
across stone, a cincture
of each distant township
tighter to this centre.

They came with light
gauged step across even
cement planks, past wide
open Midwestern barn doors,
took notice of a feeble electric
glow that backlit stained
glass windows, faced up and
into cloud shelves crossed
by the lights strung above
nearby Pere Marquette Street.

Here, they'd come to catch
the detritus of long shifts
in auto plants, the promise
at the edge of university life,
hustle favour from men
fed through an all American
political machine. Tonight
in the reticent approach
of a stale spring storm, empty
upturned lights reflect
a chorus of swallow chatter.

This station, decades shuttered,
awaits no new arrivals, greets
the last light of day scooped
from a drizzle heavy sky. With
rain shall come unseen shoots.

Geography of Peaks,
and Dips, and Lights

Lana Spendl

L EANING OVER ME TO look out the airplane window, my mother
pointed at the mountains surrounding Sarajevo. "Look! Look!"
she said. Moments before, she had been a middle-aged woman leafing
through a magazine with her glasses low on her nose. Now, she was like
a child at a household doorway, excited at the arrival of a long-awaited
family friend.

Nervousness rushed through me. I glanced out the window to sat-
isfy her—at shades of green, at patches of pines tumbling down moun-
tains—and then turned to the headrest of the woman in front of me. I
breathed in, but the air went down shaky. It could not fill me. A year
before, at sixteen, I had started doing breathing meditations in my bed-
room in Florida. Connecting to the breath often steadied me, but the
wavelets of anxiety that rose and fell in my torso now grew turbulent.
We were about to begin our descent. All around us, people talked and
laughed, languid at reaching their journey's end. A small boy stood to
his feet on his father's lap—the father held his waist with big hands—and
stretched his neck to look to the back of the plane.

Later, when we exited the airport, my mother hurried to the line of
taxis waiting nearby. She spoke to a driver, struck a deal. She direct-
ed me and the bags. The afternoon was a glare of sun. Light shone off
windshields, warmed the pavement. Across the road from the airport
lay a parking lot and beyond it a neighborhood of buildings two or three
stories high. Up above stretched a blue sky. I glanced at the beads of
sweat on the driver's bald skull, at his friendly eyes, at his shoo-shooing
hand that waved me away when I tried to lift the bags myself into the
trunk. All around, people walked and talked and gesticulated with their
arms. Some were impatient and loud. Some cracked jokes and patted
each other's backs.

I felt like myself and not myself. My home language sprung from
everyone's lips, but the voices hit pitches and speeds I did not recognize.
The eyes that met mine, however friendly and kind, were the eyes of

This essay first appeared in *The Rumpus,* January 2, 2020.

strangers. Suddenly I did not know how to stand in place. I did not know what to trust. I slid into the back seat of the cab and slammed the door shut. I looked out the window with my chin up high. My jaw held the stiffness of a statue. And I wanted it to look like that. I wanted with everything inside to look like I knew what I was doing. Like I knew where I belonged.

We left Sarajevo when I was seven, due to the Bosnian war in the early 1990s. We hopped around the Balkans, settled in Spain for several years, then moved to Florida. The move from Spain to Tampa Bay was a painful one. Spain had sparkled with restaurants, people, life. Florida was empty streets in the glaring sun. Fronds on palm trees. A shirtless man on a bicycle, T-shirt hanging from shorts.

In letters to friends in Spain, I feigned cheerfulness. I spoke of tidy suburban neighborhoods, of mailboxes like the ones we had seen on shows dubbed into Spanish like *Full House*. In truth, I felt alone. I sat sad on my bed at night. In school, I struggled to pick out words from the currents of speech around me. I felt I could not measure up.

My friends in Spain wrote about visiting their families' villages, about the ups and downs of school life. I softened at their letters and glossy pictures but felt acutely that the life I had known flowed on without me. Those familiar classrooms in afternoon light. Those faces—Irene, Esther, Tamara—whose expressions and eyes and wisps of hair I knew as well as I knew my own. I felt left out by distance and time.

A few years later, I closed down. I stopped writing back. And the letters from Spain also stopped. One friend wrote again and again, even though she was not receiving replies. In her last letter, as if into a void, she said that she was not sure this was my address anymore. I felt ashamed, but still I refused to write back. Spain was a closed room in the dark. And I could no longer bear to sit within those walls.

When I released Spain, the Sarajevo of my childhood floated up. Its mountains, its bridges, its trams. Its old men playing chess on the giant chessboard in the park. I thought of New Year's celebrations. In Bosnia, Santa Claus visited us for New Year's, and every year, we went to a party at my dad's company. Santa called us kids up one by one and gave us cellophaned packages of toys and candies and colored pencils. I admired my toys through the transparent wrap. Then we walked the packages home down the banks of the River Miljacka—my mother, my father, my brother, and I—and I breathed out hard into the cold air and marveled that my body was making clouds.

I started cradling the memory of Bosnia through tough Florida high school nights. It glowed inside me like a primordial touchstone. Through loneliness, through fights with my parents, it was the one thing undeniably mine. And then, as I was finishing my junior year in high school, my mother stood in my bedroom doorway and said that we were going back. On a visit to my grandmother, just the two of us. The winds left my lungs. I had, of course, dreamed of a someday-return—warm reconciliation, walks through cobbled streets and parks—but that someday was not now. Bosnia needed to stay buried inside, precious in the dark. But now it was coming at me at a speed I could not control. It would be around me all at once, on every side.

The night we arrived, we sat round the coffee table in my grandmother's apartment in the Grbavica neighborhood. The curtains inflated and fell with evening breeze. The wallpaper—cream, with swirls of roses—generated memories of lamplit nights and running around as a child. Up above, a hole pierced the ceiling, from a bullet that had whizzed through the window years before.

My grandmother had had her hair done in preparation for our visit. Short, curled, red as always. She pressed it to her scalp with her palms to make sure it stayed in place. She sat close to me on the couch and gazed at my face. How big I had gotten. How pretty I was. She had not seen me in several years, not since she had been in Florida. I was her first-born grandchild. Was I hungry still? I had polished off two bowls of *bosanski lonac*—full of lamb, potatoes, cabbage, tomatoes—in the kitchen when we arrived. The trip must have left me famished, poor child.

Inside me, sadness, tenderness, and fear stirred, but my body became a container, holding everything tight. I averted my eyes from hers and from my mother's. And fantasies of life back in Florida started running through my mind. My friends at lunchtime. The teacher on whom I had a crush. The narratives unfolded alongside the present moment, and I intoxicated myself with their storylines, only to come back to the living room for seconds at a time and then again retreat back.

My mother kneeled on the elaborate rug and pulled gifts out—dresses, nightgowns—from her suitcase. Leaning forward, my grandmother said that it was all too much, that she shouldn't have. But her eyes grew intent, curious. She hurried the garments to her bedroom and came out in each one and spun for us. She looked down at herself and pressed an excited hand to her mouth. Afterwards, she said she would save the pieces for a special occasion and she refolded them and slid them into plastic bags.

"What special occasion?" my mother asked. "I bought them for you to wear now."

Later that night, I retired into the bedroom my grandmother had arranged for me, and I turned off the lights. In the darkness, relief came. The outlines of the bed, the wardrobe, and the nightstand stood clear in the shadows, without the veil of fantasy now. I could breathe full again. No one's eyes studied my movements anymore.

I snuggled into the scented pillowcase and closed my eyes. But sleep did not come. Moonlight glowed faint through the windows—my grandmother's apartment perched on the seventh floor of a tall building—and softly, I rose and walked over barefoot and pulled the curtains open. Outside, Sarajevo stretched wide. A geography of peaks and dips and lights. And the same landscape swelled up to meet it from deep within my past. Dark expanses, buildings, slow headlights, riverbanks. I stood a second in disbelief. I felt displaced in time. Moments before, if I had been asked to remember Sarajevo at night, I would have gone blank. But here it was. A landscape inside me that matched what lived outside. Tears warmed my eyes, and I wiped them with fingers and covered my face with my hands. I looked out the window again, and there it still was.

The first week we walked streets lined with trees. We bought *kifle* at the corner bakery and carried their warm softness to my grandmother's place in bags. We sat with her in the kitchen in the mornings and sipped coffee from miniature cups. In the afternoons, we shopped the city and sat at tables outside restaurants and watched people pass. Passersby ran into friends with exclamations and hugs, and I withdrew a bit each time, aware that I could not walk these streets and run into anyone. Around us, bullet holes still pockmarked some buildings. Here and there, blasts of darkness colored walls. My eyes turned from these remnants of the past and focused instead on cobbles, on pigeons, on the men on the bench having a chat.

And then one afternoon, over coffee and Turkish delights, my mother suggested that we visit Vrelo Bosne. She said that I had liked it so much as a child. And a resistance swelled inside me. It made my chest wall tight. In my memory, the park glowed with fresh green and water and sun. We had visited it on weekends when I was a child. A spring broke through the earth there, and creeks roamed the grass. White swans walked and opened their wings and swam.

With single buildings in the city, I thought, I could avert my eyes. They were faceless, part of a mass. I associated little with them individually. But this park. It played like a fairytale in my mind. I would have been content to never face it again, to carry its memory, untouched, for all my life. But the thought of going had lit my mother up. Moreover, she was offering me a sweet in her mind, something she thought would delight me. Deflated, I thought I could not decline. I wanted to give her that. And so early one morning, we took the tram out.

Vrelo Bosne sits on the outskirts of Sarajevo. A walkway lined with trees leads to it, and visitors walk it or bike it or take a horse-drawn carriage down to the park. When we reached the start of the walkway, carriages stood to the side. The horses swung their tails and nodded up and down. Morning air drifted fresh with the scent of manure. Up above, the sky opened without a cloud.

My mother and I headed out on foot—she ahead, I behind. On the walkway, at the start, a sign warned visitors not to head into the field to the left due to still-active mines. My thoughts scattered. My step faltered, I almost stopped. I looked around, unsure of where to turn suddenly. Unsure of what to do now. My mother, unaffected, continued down the walkway. Had she seen the sign? Everyone, in fact, chatted or laughed or smoked cigarettes or looked out. As if the warning were just a traffic sign.

The morning chill, the carriages, the country smells all moved around me still, but the words had broken glass. I trembled—perhaps not visibly, perhaps only inside my skin, but all over, all over—and I could not tell if fear had overtaken me or if the chill in the air had simply gotten its cold fingers inside. I had been right, I thought, my childhood memories would be wiped out. My eyes fell to the ground, and dejected, I followed my mom.

We walked and walked, perhaps a few kilometers. My heart beat fast, my lungs worked hard. But the adrenaline did not lift my mood. To our right, though the line of trees, fields sloped up and down. Red-roofed country houses peppered them. I kept my head in duty down.

And then we reached the park, and I halted when I looked out. Greenness expanded in all directions. It was the freshness of young leaves, and they burst from every branch. With the foothills of Mount Igman lying nearby, waters broke the ground and ran through the grass.

Quaint bridges covered the creeks, the water glistening beneath them. Water that moved like liquid glass. White swans drifted across the surface and dipped their beaks in. And the sun that filled the space was the sun of memory. It was like no other sun. Figures glowed, children ran. The pressure in my chest—the pressure which had bound my entire being to that one spot—loosened and drifted apart. I opened to my whole body, to my eyes. My mother stood silent by my side. We remained there a while and then strolled and found a bench and sat.

I became myself, but myself in a humble, happy way. I thought: how was it still here, still here, just as it had been once? Other things had gone. Buildings, people—even us, we had gone, too—but this dream still moved and played and unfolded its light. A light that filled everything, that grew lush trees and grass. It enveloped my face, the skin of my arms. The water—cold, fresh—still burst from the ground. And the people who strolled the paths were not the strangers of the streets of Sarajevo. They were part of this, like I was. We were all part.

Hours later—tired, sated, warm—we decided to head back. My mother, spent from the sun, said that we should take a carriage. She spoke to an old driver in a cap, and we climbed up onto the red velvet seat in the back. The man rocked the carriage when he stepped to sit in front of us. Then he clicked his tongue, and the animal, muscles large, lurched forward and clip clopped on.

We did not speak the whole time. People walked by, in the direction of the park, but the crowd dwindled now. Single people here and there, a couple in conversation, a slow bicyclist. I relaxed against the cushioned seat and gazed at the country houses to the side. They stood tall, solid, white. Lots of space between them. And I imagined that I lived in one. Inside one of those houses with its steep staircase to the second floor, inside the bedroom upstairs with its window imbedded in the thick wall. Looking out at fields and sky. And I became a young woman in old Bosnia. The afternoon opened, time slowed down. And it was not the time of future or past. The world settled into something present, ever present, something I trusted like the hands of a wise, old aunt. It moved at its pace, of its own accord. It carried me in its placid arms. And I did not have the urge to fight. I could allow. Then snippets of life sprung up. Bounding down the stairs in bare feet. Slipping into shoes at the entrance of the house. Pulling shut the wooden door and heading to the village gathering across the grass.

Mujeres / **Women**

Marjorie Agosín

Las mujeres, siempre las que aguardan
A la salida de las ciudades,
En los caminos tormentosos,
Las que aguardan llegadas
De los hijos de la guerra,
Las que aguardan en las orillas
De todos los caminos secos,
De los ríos con piedras secas,
Como la misma agua seca.

Aguardan llegadas,
Traen mantas para cubrir a los hijos que sobreviven,
A los hijos que no llegan,
Siempre aguardando
Entre la luz y la sombra,
Entre los vientos de la desgracia,
Entre los memoriales del olvido.
Aguardan …

Son mujeres de agua,
Son mujeres de trigo,
Siempre son mujeres
En las orillas de los caminos,
En los senderos de la memoria,
Mujeres acariciando a un niño por nacer,
Meciéndolo, cántandole, brindándole falsas promesas
De un porvenir azul.
Con esos hijos pronto a nacer
Aguardan el día de la luz …
Y solas los reciben,
Y solas con ellos
Bordan la historia de un nuevo mundo.

Las mujeres buscando a esos hijos desvalidos,
Los que cruzaron los ríos de las secas gargantas,
Los que ya no son ni historia ni piedras,
Para rescatarlos del olvido.

Las mujeres enamoradas,
Aquellas dulces mujeres con sabor a río dulce,
Las que sentadas sobre las riberas
Esperan el tiempo de una sola caricia.
Las mujeres que esperan un solo beso,
Las mujeres que esperan que ya no serán golpeadas,
Que no serán mutiladas,
Las que esperan que vuelva el esposo sin castigos,
Las mujeres que quieren un instante de amor,
El reconocimiento de una mirada,
El instante de la inquietud del alma,
Las que quieren ser miradas por lo que son,
Las que quieren que alguien sea el lector de sus almas.

Las mujeres ancianas que velan por sus hijas
Para que nadie les corte el corazón,
Para que nadie las mutile
Y las deje a las orillas de los ríos secos …

Las mujeres rezando por sus muertos,
Las mujeres rezando por sus vivos,
Las mujeres en el tiempo de la vigilia y el sueño,
Las mujeres desesperadas frente al desamor,
Las mujeres del mundo unidas por una sonrisa,
Unas manos que acarician
Unos labios que hablan otros lenguajes,
Unas manos que esperan para abrazar.

Somos eso,
Las mujeres nobles, guardianes de la memoria,
Dulces en la espera,
Las mujeres que aman en los perdidos páramos de la memoria,
Las mujeres reconociendo el rostro de sus amados,
Las mujeres esperando un tren, un navío, una palabra, una caricia, un
    vientecito claro …
Las mujeres que aguardan la noche y el día,
Las radiantes mujeres que a ti te esperan en los senderos de luz,
Las mujeres que se levantan desde entre las marejadas y las grandes espumas
Para mirar las costas,
El privilegiado horizonte de la vida.

Women are always the ones who wait
On the outskirts of cities,
On tempestuous paths.
They await the arrival
Of the children of war,
They wait on the side of arid roads,
On riverbanks of dry rocks,
Like the parched water itself.

They await an arrival,
They bring blankets to cover the children who survive
And those who never come home.
They are always waiting
Amid the light and the shadows,
Amid the winds of misfortune,
Amid memorials of oblivion.
They wait …

They are women made of water,
They are women made of wheat.
It is always the women
On the sides of roads,
On the paths of memory,
Women caressing their unborn children,
Rocking them, singing to them, making them false promises
Of a blue future.
With those children soon to be born,
The women await the day they will give birth …
And they welcome the children alone,
And alone with them
They embroider the story of a new world.

The women search for those helpless children
Who crossed the rivers with parched throats,
Who are no longer stories or stones,
To save them from oblivion.

Women in love,
Those sweet women who taste like a sweet river,
Women who sit on the shores
Awaiting the promise of a single caress,
Women who yearn for a single kiss,
Women who hope they will no longer be beaten,
That they will not be maimed.
They await their husbands hoping not to be punished,
Women who crave a moment of love,
Acknowledgement in a glance,
A stirring in their souls,
Who want to be seen for who they are,
Who want someone to read their souls.

Elderly women who watch over their daughters
So no one slashes their hearts,
So no one mutilates them
And leaves them on the banks of arid rivers …

Women praying for their dead,
Women praying for their living,
Women in the time of wakefulness and dreams,
Women desperate in the face of heartbreak,
Women of the world united by a smile,
By hands that caress,
By lips that speak other languages,
By hands that wait to embrace.

That is who we women are:
The noble guardians of memory
Who lovingly wait,
Women who love in the lost heaths of memory,
Women who recognize the faces of their loved ones,
Women awaiting a train, a ship, a word, a caress, a clear breeze …
Women who wait for night and day,
Radiant women who wait for you on the paths of light,
Women who stand up from amid the swells and the mighty waves
To spy the shore,
The privileged horizon of life.

(Translated from Spanish by Alison Ridley.)

Sanchez across the Street

Bárbara Mujica

WHEN THE SANCHEZ FAMILY moved into the house across the street—the one that had been owned by the Schapiros—things went from bad to worse.

We lived on a small street with a Spanish name—half the streets in Los Angeles have Spanish names—near Fairfax Avenue. A casual passer-by might miss the *mezuzah*[1] on the right doorpost of every house, but the mailman knew the make-up of the neighborhood. On the corner, the Bravermans. Then the Langs, the Zimmermans, the Meisners, the Gattliebs, the Weinbergs, the Schapiros, the Goldsteins, and the Horowitzes. On one side of us lived Harry Rabbinowitz, his mother, his wife Anne, and the four Rabbinowitz girls. On the other side lived the Friedmans—Ben and Ethel and their kids Rachel and Jonathan. We were the Rivkins—Abe, Rose, Leah (my older sister), Amy (me), Aaron, and Gail.

Leah was the family brain. She was the kind of kid who took all the hardest subjects. Other kids took French or Spanish to meet their foreign language requirement. Leah took Russian.

Other kids took math through algebra. Leah went on to trigonometry. She was like a bulldog. Once she decided to do something, there was no backing down. I could never compete with Leah, and I gave up trying sometime around the third grade. I was the B student, the editor of the yearbook, the president of the Spirit Club.

Aaron was the school clown. He was the kid who stuck wads of gum on the teacher's seat. Once, he borrowed a motorbike from a friend. Vrrrroom! Up and down the venerated halls of Fairfax High School, the best public high school in Los Angeles, charged Aaron Rivkin, terror of the Borscht Belt (the name Gentiles gave to the Fairfax Avenue area). Vrrrrooooom! Up the stairs he went on his motorized assault steed. Vrrrroom! The boys yelled and applauded, and the girls broke into a

---

1   The spellings of Yiddish words commonly used in English are from *The Random House Dictionary of the English Language*. The spellings of other Yiddish words are from Herman Galvin and Stan Tamarkin, *The Yiddish Dictionary Sourcebook* (Ktav Publishing House, 1986).

cheerleading routine, and Mr. Arnot, the boys vice principal, turned the color of an eggplant. He suspended Aaron for two days. "Oy, if only this kid would apply himself," Mom used to say, "he could be a lawyer or a politician. He's got the *chutzpa*." "Or even the President!" Dad would add. "Or even the Pope!" Aaron would hoot, standing up on Mom's kitchen stool and waving an unfurled napkin like a banner.

Gail's distinction was that she had more pictures of movie stars than any other girl at Bancroft Junior High School. During various phases her room was plastered with pictures of Elvis Presley, Pat Boone, and later, the Beatles—the kind of pictures you got from *Dig* magazine by sending in a large self-addressed stamped envelope and a dollar. Gail was always "going steady" with somebody—usually boys who rarely called and never came by, but who played the lead in the endless dramas she described to her girlfriends over the phone. Her notebooks were filled with junior high graffiti: Steve loves Beth; Sue loves Harvey; Gail loves ~~Bill~~, ~~Mark~~, Jim. "She should fall for Down the Street's kid," said Mom. "Such a little doll. Straight A's he gets."

Mother referred to people by their place on the block. For example, "Braverman on the corner bought a new sofa, but they didn't have the color beige she wanted, so she had to settle for green." Or else, Weinberg across the street told me she was going to start working at May Company a couple of days a week. Minkoff around the block is going to babysit her kids." Or else, "Lang by Braverman has to have her ovaries removed." Sometimes the name would disappear altogether, as in, "Around the corner called me this afternoon. She says her Barbara is going with across the street by Meisner to the prom. Next door says he got into Berkeley." It was up to the listener to figure out that "he" referred to Carl, the son of Jill and Ralph Gottlieb, who lived next to the Meisners across the street.

"This neighborhood," my father would say, "has too goddamn many Jews. It's a bad situation."

"Oy, again he's *kvetshing*. Abe, please. What's so terrible that it's a Jewish neighborhood?"

"They make you *meshugana*, these people with their *bar mitzvahs* and their dinner parties and their *meshugaas*. Always showing off. That's what they are, Jews. Showoffs."

But that wasn't the real problem. The real problem was that Dad wanted to be American, really American, and to his mind, Jews were immigrants. He wanted to live in a neighborhood where people had names like Smith and Livingston and spoke in the soft tones that Dad associated with Protestants—the ladies with blue hair and DAR credentials who lived in the Highland Avenue area. Loud noises, as far as Dad was concerned, were the mark of those who twenty years later would be labeled "ethnics." Dad wasn't a snob. Not really. On a one-on-one basis, he liked nearly everybody. But Dad was obsessed with assimilation. On the night our high school sponsored a "heritage" dinner in which all of the students were supposed to bring typical dishes from their country of origin, Dad showed up with six pounds of Swift's premium hot dogs and a huge jar of mustard. Dad himself had been born in Jersey City and had played baseball as a boy.

"Look," he'd say if you reminded him that he had roots in Minsk, "I'm from Jersey. I played baseball. Baseball, the all-American game, goddamn it! Right out there in the empty lot by Baroni's grocery, along with Phil Marcus, Tom O'Riley and Eddie Balducci. And even Ronnie Fairweather, see? Even Ronnie Fairweather. His father came over on the goddamn *Mayflower*! I was a great hitter. A great hitter! And another thing: I danced the lindy and the foxtrot. You think I danced the goddamn *hora*, when I was a kid? I danced to Benny Goodman!"

Most of the others—Braverman, Horowitz, Rabbinowitz, Schapiro—had come from Russia or Germany or Poland after the war. Dad liked them. I would even say that Dad loved them. There wasn't anything that he wouldn't do for them. He wired their houses and fixed their circuits and never charged any of them a dime. He drove their wives to the hospital to have babies and sat up all night with the prospective father in the waiting room, smoking cigarette after cigarette. He attended their sons' *bar mitzvahs*, he helped them make arrangements for their daughters' weddings. He listened to their problems. He lent them money in a pinch. And yet, these people weren't the all-American types that Dad yearned to be neighbors with. They had accents and stuck with the old ways. On Saturday, they walked back from the synagogue with *yarmulkes* on their heads. "So what's the big deal, Abe?" Mom would say. "My mother and father spoke with an accent. Your mother and father spoke with an accent ... ."

What the neighborhood needed, Dad thought, was some Protestants. Not Catholics. Catholics would probably be Irish or Polish or Italian, or, God forbid, Mexican. To Dad's mind, Catholics were no more real Americans than Jews were.

Estrangement

Dad's name was Abraham Rivkin, and he was an electrician. He had a shop on Larchmont Boulevard and received a lot of business from the ladies who lived in the huge, Spanish-style houses behind Highland Avenue. These were fabulous homes with sprawling lawns, wrought-iron gates, patios and terraces embellished with oleanders, roses, hollyhocks, and fragrant trees—lemon, orange, olive, quince. For professional purposes, Dad used the name Conrad Greer, which had a nice ring to it and would, he thought, please a clientele disinclined to do business with an electrician named Abe Rivkin.

Occasionally, someone would call the house and ask to talk to Mr. Greer, and, if my mother answered, she would say something like, "Oy, vey, this man is meshugana with his fancy names. Abe, it's for you!" And Dad, who was afraid that the caller had heard her, would yell, "Would you shut up, Rose!", and my mother would scowl and say, "Please, Abe. Act like a mensch and don't use dirty language in front of the children."

My brother Aaron and my two sisters, Leah and Gail, would burst out laughing, and Mom would shrug her shoulders, but Dad would close the door to the hall where the telephone was so that his caller couldn't hear us.

Mom didn't share Dad's prejudices. She liked the neighborhood and was friendly with all the women up and down the street. She walked to synagogue with them on Friday night, even though she didn't care for what she called "all that religious rigmarole" and didn't believe half of what the rabbi said.

It was a cohesive group. If Mrs. Goldstein was sick, Mrs. Lang would cook for her family. If Mrs. Zimmerman's car broke down, Mrs. Rabbinowitz would drive her kids to school. Mom did for everyone, and everyone was welcome in our house. These were people who had lived through situations in which, if you didn't stick together, you might not survive, and so, they helped each other gladly, without being asked and without exacting compensation.

Mom liked the neighborhood for other reasons as well. It was within walking distance of Fairfax Avenue, where she worked as a receptionist in the mornings at a discount beauty shop. Mrs. Braverman and Mrs. Meisner had their hair cut there, and so did Mrs. Minkoff around the block. At the shop, Mom learned the local gossip and did a few good deeds. When the daughter of the black cleaning lady fell off her bike and broke her tooth, Mom went home to get her car and drove all the way over to South San Gabriel to pick up the child and get her to a dentist. And when the wife of the night janitor—also black—died of cancer, Mom cooked for the family for two weeks.

In the afternoons, Mom could stop at the kosher butcher's, the deli, the cleaner's and the Safeway, all near Fairfax Avenue. The butcher and the deli would deliver, and Mom would bring the groceries home from the Safeway in a little metal cart that she had purchased for the purpose. Mom didn't like to drive because traffic made her nervous; she got behind the wheel only when circumstances forced her to.

Mom bought from Katz, the kosher butcher, because she liked to gossip with him and because she thought that he had better meat than the Safeway, "although the Safeway is good," she told me confidentially. "Better than Ralph's on Third Street. But fresh like Katz's, you can't find meat anywhere in the city."

Mom didn't keep a kosher kitchen. For one thing, we all liked bacon. For another, to her, the dietary laws made no sense at all "in this day and age" and "in a clean country, like the United States." Mrs. Lang, who did keep a kosher kitchen and was at our house one day when Mom was explaining her position, said that Mom was absolutely right, but, "What can I do, Rose? My husband is a traditionalist. So?"

"So do it his way and keep peace in the family."

"That's exactly right, Rose. Bickering and fighting over something so stupid as this dish is for *milkh* and that dish is for *fleysh*, who needs it? You know what I mean? Better just to do it his way."

"Right. Here, take another *kikhl*."

"Thanks. These are delicious, Rose."

"From Katz's wife Sadie. She bakes. Because there is enough misery in life, without looking for more. So if he wants a special dish for *milkh*, let him have it, Bessie, even if you don't believe in all that *meshugaas*. What's the difference? How much extra work is it to keep an extra set of dishes?"

"That's what I say."

Once a week Mom and Mrs. Braverman went down to UCLA to take a course. Mom liked to go with the neighbor because Mrs. Braverman didn't mind driving. There was no logic or order to the courses Mom enrolled in, but she took them all very seriously and always got A's. One semester she took a course called Forming Public Opinion. Another semester she studied the modern history of the Middle East. Her favorite course was ethnomusicology, which was taught by a handsome Iranian named Farhat who sat on pillow and played the zither. One evening, Mom invited him to dinner. She made stuffed cabbage and served no wine because she knew it was against his religion. After we ate, he sat on the floor and entertained us for hours.

"So, he's a Moslem," she said. "So what? He's a cultured man. Why shouldn't I have him in my house? We can learn from him and he can learn from us."

Rose Frieda Rivkin was a sensible woman. Everyone said so. That's why Aaron, Leah, Gail, and I couldn't figure out why she was carrying on so much about Sanchez across the street.

The news that Esther and Morris Schapiro were selling their house had surprised no one. Esther and Morris had lived in the neighborhood for ages. In fact, they had been among the first Jewish residents, having moved in just when the area was beginning to "turn" from Irish. But now they were older, and the house had gotten to be too much for Esther, who had a heart condition. The Schapiro's only daughter had graduated college and married a chiropractor. ("*Sheyne meydl*, bless her!") The young couple now had a child of their own and a place in Santa Monica, and so Esther and Morris had decided that there was no point in hanging onto a house that had begun to be a burden. The stucco walls were cracking. The wiring was in need of repair. The flagstones in the patio had grass growing between them, and honeysuckle was overgrowing the roses. The Schapiros put their house on the market and added their names to the waiting list at the Park La Brea Towers, an apartment complex for seniors.

Eight months later, the Sanchez family—eleven kids, three dogs, two parents, and a grandmother—were moving in. They had the most disorderly, dilapidated array of belongings that anyone on our street had ever seen—sofas and chairs that didn't match, phony baroque lamps and tables with cherubs and flowers stamped all over, paintings on black velvet of bullfighters in bright colors, broken down bicycles that had obviously been passed from one child to the next, and crucifixes. Crucifixes!

Mom stood at the living-room window and wept.

The Sanchezes hadn't used a professional moving company. Instead, they had rented a van, and the Sanchez men and boys were hauling heavy furniture onto the lawn, while the Sanchez women sorted domestic artifacts on the porch. Three or four laughing children raced through the mess, leaping from the cab of the van onto the street and skipping over beds and boxes as though these objects formed an obstacle course.

"*Oy, vey.* Like animals they live," Mom said.

Mom kept her living room impeccable. It was not for living at all. Each chair and sofa was carefully guarded with a plastic cover, which was removed only when we had guests. On the wall there was a painting of the English countryside that my parents had bought at an auction, and my mother dusted the frame daily. She also dusted the coffee tables, the lamps, the piano and bench, the bookshelves and the bric-a-brac that she had accumulated over the years—a statuette of a woman dressed like Martha Washington, a Limoges cup and saucer, a ceramic bird, a French music box. My sisters and brother and I were allowed in the living room only to practice our piano lessons.

The sight of the Sanchezes' shabby, mismatched upholstery was making Mom ill. Her breathing became irregular and she started to hiccup.

Dad came up and stood behind her.

"*Oy, oy, oy,*" he said. From his tone, you would have thought that he had just received notice of the death of a favorite uncle. "Did you ever see such *khazeray*? This neighborhood is going from bad to worse."

By now, we were all crowding behind Mom, trying to get a look at the Sanchezes.

"Eleven kids! My God, eleven!"

"Look at that sofa! I bet they got it from the Salvation Army!"

"Where are they going to put all of those people? There are only three bedrooms in the house."

"Four, if you count the den in the back. They could use that as a bedroom."

"Look at all the little kids. Maybe I could get a babysitting job."

"Yeah, Leah, like they really need a babysitter with all those teenagers and the granny, too." Aaron pinched her arm and grinned that winning grin of his that always made Leah change her mind whenever she was about to bop him.

"You stay away from those people, Leah," snapped Dad. "And you, too, Gail. And you, too, Amy." He looked right at me when he said my name.

Dad was nervous and jealous at the same time. Of the eleven Sanchez children, nine were boys.

"So many sons," he said wistfully. "How come Jews never have so many sons?"

And then, as if remembering once again the threat that so many young men—young *Latin* men, with all the hot blood that the word implies—posed to his own family, Dad repeated his warning:

"Amy, Leah, Gail, keep clear of those people. You hear me?"

"Why, Daddy?" asked Gail.

Dad paused, as if the answer were too obvious even to articulate, although all of us knew that he was trying to think of something convincing to say.

"They're dangerous."

"Why, Daddy? Why are they dangerous?" Dad walked out of the room.

"How could she do this to us?" Mother wailed. "Who?" asked Leah.

Gail, who was twelve, scrutinized a young man in low-slung jeans. He had smooth black hair and broad shoulders and skin the color of tea. He was lowering a painting off the van, and his arms were tensed to show his muscles to the best advantage.

"Isn't he dreamy, Amy?" Gail whispered to me.

I signaled her to be quiet. But Aaron had heard and began to laugh.

"I'm gonna tell Dad!" he teased.

"You do and I'll ... I'll ... I'll flush your goldfish down the toilet!"

"I just don't understand how she could do it to us," sighed Mom.

"Who, Mom?" asked Leah again. "How could who do what to us?"

"My, God," Mom said in disgust. "Now they're going to stink up the schools."

Fairfax High School was the pride of the neighborhood. It had one of the highest rates of college acceptance for its seniors. It was almost entirely Jewish.

"Who, Mom? How could who do what to us?"

"Across the street. After all these years."

"Who across the street, Mom?"

"Who do you think across the street, Leah? Who are we talking about?"

"I don't know, Mom. A Mexican family lives across the street now."

"*Oy, vey!* Such a mouth on this kid. Don't get smart with me, Leah. Schapiro across the street. How could she sell her beautiful house to that Mexican *shmuts* and ruin the neighborhood? Who would have thought that Connie Schapiro would sell her house to *guyim?* A member of Hadassah, yet. A medal she got last year–for being a long-standing member of Hadassah. And him. In *B'nai Brith* since as long as I can remember."

"They're not going to ruin the neighborhood, Mom," laughed Aaron. "A few hot peppers will spice this street up! Anyhow, the Schapiros had to sell their house. They had it on the market for eight months and their apartment came through in Park La Brea Towers. Be reasonable, Mom."

"Mexicans," said Mom, paying no attention to Aaron. "They're worse than *shvarts.* Like animals. Who has eleven kids today?"

"*Bobe* and *Zeyde* had eleven kids."

"That's different, Gail. It was all right then, but it's not all right now. When my mother was young, everyone had big families. People didn't know how to control their ... their ... those things."

"*Bobe* Rivkin had nine kids."

"That's what I'm telling you, Gail. Everyone had big families back then."

"So, what you're saying, Mom, is that there's nothing intrinsically wrong with big families."

"Don't get smart with me, Aaron! Just don't you open a mouth to me!"

No one had realized just how upset Mom really was until she turned her face away from the window, tears streaming down her cheeks, and walked out of the room. It was her neighborhood, the only one she had known since she moved to Los Angeles from New Jersey in the late 1940s, and she loved it just the way it had been all these years. And now, to her mind, it was falling apart.

The Sanchez children enrolled in the neighborhood schools: Fairfax High School, Bancroft Junior High School, Rosewood Elementary School. The brood spanned seventeen years, so there were Sanchez children who were out working at the same time that there were Sanchez children still in strollers.

Leah and I hardly saw them. Leah was seventeen, a senior. I was a year younger. We were both in high school, in fast-track courses. We had expected the Sanchez kids to be placed in remedial reading and shop, but Aaron, who, the very first day had gone across the street in full view of his father to welcome the new family, told us that they were all in regular, middle-track classes. Except Johnny. Johnny Sanchez was in honors math. Aaron, like the older Sanchez girl, Neli, was a sophomore, and they were in history class together.

Aaron was a smart kid, the smartest of her children, Mom used to say. He was not a motivated student, and so he was never in the honors classes, but he was a whiz at repairing things and could do calculations better than any of us. "He could have been an engineer," Mom said years later, when it was too late. "An engineer, not a lawyer or a politician. That's what he was cut out to be."

"The one with the … The one who was taking the picture down … what's his name?" Gail asked Aaron over dinner. Dad wasn't at the table. He was out working somewhere, fixing somebody's wiring.

"The one you were staring at?"

"Shut up, you jerk! I wasn't staring!"

"Suit yourself, you boy-crazy little spaz. His name is Vince. Too old for you, though. He's seventeen. And don't forget, you're only twelve."

Gail shot her older brother a look full of venom and sank into a sulk. Aaron leaned over and mussed her hair, and she spit a mouthful of mashed potatoes at him and then burst out laughing. He pretended to punch her stomach, then wiped the potatoes off his eyebrow.

During those first few months after the new family moved in, none of us girls ever ventured over to the Sanchez house. For us, it was off-limits. But Aaron was over there every day. He and the Sanchez boys tinkered with cars, played ball in the driveway, or listened to music. That is how we came to be the first Jews on the block who knew, before anyone else even cared, that Ritchie Valens' real name was Valenzuela.

"What's he do?" Mom asked Aaron one night after dinner.

"Who?"

"Sanchez across the street."

"He has a grocery store."

"He owns it or he works in it?"

"He owns it."

"A *makher*," said Dad, without looking up from his pot roast.

"Over in East LA."

"So why doesn't he live in East LA like the rest of them?"

"If you had the choice, would you rather live in East LA or here?" asked Aaron.

Mom didn't answer. She just got up to pour herself another cup of tea.

"What's it like over there?" she asked when she sat down again.

"Just like over here," said Aaron. "Only noisier."

"Because they're Mexicans."

"No," said Aaron. "Because there are more of them. By the way, not all of those kids are Mr. Sanchez's. Five of them are his brother's. His brother was killed in an accident in Mexico."

Mom looked up from her tea. She was sensitive to misfortune.

"By a tractor, on a farm where he was working. And the mother just couldn't manage all the kids, so the Sanchezes across the street took in the whole bunch, and they're raising them as their own."

"Wow," said Leah. "You have to be practically a saint to do something like that."

"That's really something," added Gail. "Is Vince Mr. Sanchez's son or his nephew?"

Mom didn't say anything for a long time, but we could tell she was moved. Finally, she spoke: "You don't have to be Jewish to be a *mensch*, you know. A Mexican can be a *mensch*."

"But they're still Mexicans," said Dad.

"Yes," Mom said. "They're still Mexicans."

Mom spent a lot of time watching the Sanchezes across the street. Before, she had rarely gone into the living room, except to clean. But the living-room window offered the best view of the Sanchez house, and so now, she would stand for long periods—fifteen or twenty minutes—dustcloth in hand, watching Mrs. Sanchez and her mother-in-law planting pansies and pulling back honeysuckles while children skipped rope in the driveway.

Soon the garden looked better than it had in years.

"Why don't you tell her?" suggested Aaron. "Why don't you go over and tell Mrs. Sanchez how nice her flowers look? She'd really like to hear it from you. No one in the neighborhood has gone over there to meet her."

Mom shook her head and began to dust in earnest.

But one day the following week, when Mom and I were coming home from shopping, Mrs. Sanchez, who, as usual, was working in her yard, waved to us.

"Hi," said Mom. "Nice flowers."

"Thanks," called Mrs. Sanchez, smiling widely.

That evening, Aaron went across the street to study with Johnny, who was the only kid in the neighborhood who was quicker than he in algebra. He came back with a huge plate of *enchiladas*.

"Here," he said to Mom. "Mrs. Sanchez wants us to try these." Mom looked at them as if they were excrement, and I was sure that she was going to throw them in the garbage. But at dinnertime, she set them on the table, a little to the side like an uninvited guest, along with the baked chicken and a salad. "What's this?" asked Dad.

"From Sanchez across the street," said Mom.

"They're called *enchiladas*," explained Aaron.

"Looks like *blintzes*," said Dad.

Leah took a spatula and lifted up an *enchilada*, dripping thick red sauce back into the serving dish.

"It's good!" she declared after taking a bite.

"I know," said Aaron. "Mrs. Sanchez is a great cook, and so is Grandma Sanchez."

Mom looked disgusted.

"You eat there? You've eaten these things before?"

"Oh, sure! *Enchiladas* and *tacos* and *chiles rellenos* ... Have one, Mom."

Mom wouldn't try Mrs. Sanchez's *enchiladas*, although the rest of us did—even Dad. By the end of the meal, we had eaten them all, as well as Mom's baked chicken, which we were afraid to leave, lest Mom take offense.

"Tell her thank you," Mom said to Aaron as she washed the serving dish to send back to Mrs. Sanchez. "Tell her they were very good."

The next time she made *blintzes*, Mom sent three dozen of them over to the Sanchezes.

"*Oy*, such a big family," she said as she mixed the batter. This will cost a fortune."

But she made the paper-thin pancakes and filled them with cheese one by one without further complaint. Then she placed the *blintzes* in a Pyrex dish and covered it with wax paper and gave it to Aaron.

"Tell her they should eat them with jam or sour cream," she instructed.

"Why don't you take them over yourself, Mom? Mrs. Sanchez always says how much she'd like to meet you."

"Another time."

"You always say that."

But Aaron didn't insist because he knew that deep down inside, it wasn't the Sanchezes that Mom resented, but the fact that the neighborhood was changing and her little world was falling apart. It was painful for her to let go.

Aaron stayed to eat Mom's *blintzes* with the Sanchezes and reported that they all enjoyed them very much.

"She tried them?" Mom wanted to know. "Who, Mom?"

"Sanchez across the street, Aaron. Who are we talking about?"

"Mrs. Sanchez?"

"Of course, Mrs. Sanchez."

"There are four females in the Sanchez family, Mom. " '*Buelita*—that's the grandmother, *abuela* means grandmother in Spanish—Mrs. Sanchez, Neli, and Lupe. How am I supposed to know who you're talking about?"

"Such a mouth on this kid. I never saw anything like it!"

"Yes, she tried them."

"With jam?"

"With sour cream."

"Mexicans know from sour cream?"

"Of course Mexicans know from sour cream, Mom. You can even put sour cream on *enchiladas*."

"Red *blintzes*, that's all they are," piped up Dad from behind the *Los Angeles Times*. "What language do they speak over there, Aaron?"

"English."

Dad put down his newspaper. "English?"

"Of course, English. They're Americans, aren't they?"

"They're Mexicans."

"They're Mexicans like we're Russian Jews, Dad."

"Don't get smart with your father, Aaron. Don't open a ... " But Dad cut her off.

"You mean they all speak English?"

"Yeah, they all speak English. Sometimes the grandmother and Mrs. Sanchez speak Spanish together, but most of the time they speak English. And the kids, they always speak English. Mr. Sanchez insists on it. He says he didn't come here to live the way lived in Mexico. He's a naturalized American citizen, Dad. He's a Republican like you, for God's sake!"

Dad looked at Aaron for a long time, then started to laugh. "Well, I'll be damned," he said, finally.

"Yeah, Dad. Mr. Sanchez is a real American. Just like you."

If Dad was insulted by the comparison, he didn't show it. He just sat there and chuckled behind his newspaper.

"What's it look like over there?" Mom wanted to know. Connie Schapiro was as neat as a pin. Even when she got sick, she kept up the house—had a *shvarts* come in once a week to clean. I'll bet they've got it plenty crapped up. I saw the *drek* they *schlepped* in when they moved."

"Mrs. Sanchez is as neat as a pin, too, Mom. And 'Buelita is always cleaning."

"And the furniture?"

"You saw it. It's old, but it looks okay the way they've got it set up. That pinkish sofa opens into a bed. That's where the little ones sleep at night."

"Oy."

"Everything has its place. It's just ... let's say ... a different style from ours."

"Yeah, I'll say."

But Mom looked relieved to know that there was some semblance of order in what had once been Connie Schapiro's living room.

Neli Sanchez was turning fifteen and her uncle, Victor Sanchez across the Street, was throwing a huge party for her. Aaron brought the news.

"It's a Mexican tradition," he said. "When a girl turns fifteen, she becomes a woman. She becomes, you know, eligible ... only not really. Neli's just a kid. She's not going to run off and get married to anyone. She wants to finish school and become a nurse. The party, it's just symbolic. You know, like a Sweet Sixteen. Anyhow, they're having a big bash. *Mariachis*, *piñatas*, the works. Relatives are coming from all over. Maybe even from Mexico."

"If they're so American," said Leah, "why don't they have a Sweet Sixteen, instead?"

"We're American, and I had a *bar mitzvah*, Miss Know-it-all." Again, the grin.

"Shut up, Aaron. You're such a brat."

"Well, the best part is, they've invited us!"

"Us?"

"Yeah, all of us, even Mom and Dad. Because when Mexicans give parties, they don't segregate people by age. They have old people, people Mom's and Dad's age, kids, teenagers, everybody. 'Buelita is going to cook her heart out, Mom. We have to go!"

"We'll see."

"C'mon, Mom. Every time you say, 'We'll see,' it means no."

"They don't even know us," said Leah. "They only know you."

"Well, they want to meet all of us, and this is our chance." Gail was prancing around like a pony.

"Can I wear my yellow dress?" she begged. "Can I?"

I really didn't think that Mom would let us go. For a long time, she changed the subject every time Aaron mentioned Neli's fifteenth birthday party.

"I have to go," Aaron announced, after Mom had beaten around the bush for more than a week, "whether the girls go or not. I'm Neli's special guest. She's going to dance the first dance with me."

"*Oy*," moaned Mom. "My Aaron dancing with a *shikse*. And a Mexican yet. I never thought I'd live to see the day. Did I raise you for this, Aaron?"

Aaron roared with laughter.

"Don't worry, Mom," he said. "We're not getting married. I promise you, I won't marry a *shikse*."

As it turned out, Aaron kept his promise. Oh God, if only he were alive and well today and married to Neli Sanchez.

Mom held off until the last minute, bringing up a million reasons why we shouldn't go. First of all, they were Mexicans, and this was to be a Mexican party, in which we had absolutely no business. And who went to parties with *goyim*? And who knew what might go on? Drinking, maybe—excessive drinking. And, *oy vey*, what would the neighbors say? What would Braverman on the corner say? And Minkoff across the street? And Rabbinowitz next door? After all, the Rabbinowitz girls weren't going, weren't even invited. So what would Harry and Anne Rabbinowitz think if the Rivkins allowed their daughters to go and dance in the arms of *goyim*? And Mexicans! What would they say at the synagogue? What would the rabbi say?"

"C'mon, Mom!" teased Aaron. "You don't care what the rabbi says. You always say he's a jerk. You didn't worry what the rabbi would say when you invited Professor Farhat to have dinner here."

Aaron was right, but still, Mom didn't feel comfortable about the whole thing. In the end, though, she said yes, although she didn't go herself. She baked her special *apfelkuchen* and bought a *punschtorte* from Katz's wife, and sent them over with us.

It was a fabulous party, with hundreds of guests filing in and out of the house and patio, bringing food, and cakes and gifts. There was a *mariachi* band whose members dressed in black, glittery outfits and red-trimmed *sombreros*. They were strong on the brass and played all the old favorites: *Cucurrucucu Paloma, Cielito lindo,* and, of course, *Las mañanitas,* as well as lots of famous *corridos* and *rancheras* whose names I don't remember. Neli was beautiful with her long, black hair braided and turned over her head, and her fluffy white dress. She danced with Aaron and with her brothers, even the little ones, and with her uncles, especially Mr. Sanchez, who had raised her since her father's death.

When Dad came to get us at about two in the morning, the party was still going strong. Mr. Sanchez asked him to come in, and Dad accepted. He stayed for about an hour, talking and laughing with Mr. Sanchez, and eating *burritos* and *enchiladas.* In the end, they were calling each other Victor and Abe and making plans to get Mr. Sanchez into the Lions Club. We left at about three, but the party continued until dawn. Mrs. Weinberg and Mrs. Goldstein, who lived on either side of the Sanchezes, had plenty to say about it the next day. Mom just shrugged and said that they were Mexicans, so what could you expect, they had their own way of doing things.

But Mom was sad because, there was no denying it now, the neighborhood had changed, and there was nothing to be done about it.

Leah graduated at the end of the school year. Mom gave a little party at home, but she didn't invite the Sanchezes. It was just a family party, she said. Just a little get-together.

In September, Leah went to UCLA to study Biology. I went the following year. Both of us lived on campus, in Hershey Hall, the only all-girls dormitory at the university. Dad would have preferred us to live at home, but Mom said the experience of having to do for ourselves would be good for us.

"They should learn what it is to iron a blouse," she said. It was just a manner of speaking. Leah and I had been ironing blouses for years.

Aaron was still in high school, and he kept us informed of the doings of the Sanchez family across the street. Thanks to Dad, Mr. Sanchez had joined the Lions Club. The two men went to meetings together one Thursday night a month. Vince Sanchez had graduated high school the same year as Leah. He was living at home and studying at Los Angeles City College. Johnny had gotten a scholarship to the California Institute of Technology. He wanted to be an engineer. Neli was applying to UCLA for the coming semester. She still hoped to become a nurse.

"They're no *schleppers*, those kids," Mom told me over the phone. "They've got *chutzpa*."

Aaron was another story.

"I wish your brother had drive like those Sanchez boys." Whenever we got together, Mom would shake her head and wring her hands a little too melodramatically, we thought at the time. "What will become of this kid, God only knows," she would say.

Aaron had decided not to go to college right after graduation. He was tired of studying, he said. He wanted to take a couple of years off, maybe work with Dad, learn the business. Then he would go back to school. He would study electrical engineering, he assured Mom, just not right away. Mom begged, but Aaron's mind was made up.

"They're all going to school," she complained. "All of them, except mine. Lang across the street, Minkoff around the block. Even Sanchez. Those Mexican kids sitting in colleges while mine fools around in his father's store. Who ever heard of such *meshugaas*? A Jewish boy turning his back on education! *Oy vey ist mir.* You could die from such nonsense."

Mom was right. It was serious business. The war was on.

In June 1964, Aaron graduated high school. He took an apartment off San Vicente Boulevard with a friend from high school named Jerry who was studying television repair.

Late in 1964, Aaron was drafted.

"Don't worry, Mom," he said. "They don't put Jews in the front lines. They put them behind desks."

"Take care of Mom," he whispered in my ear. Then he kissed me on the cheek.

"If anything happens to me, I bequeath you my goldfish," he told Gail, laughing. He hugged her tightly. Then he embraced Leah and, last of all, Dad, who was fighting back the tears.

"Don't be too much of a smartass," he said, trying to smile. "No motorbikes in the mess hall!"

"Ay, ay, Captain," said Aaron. Dad had been a captain in the Air Force during World War II.

On May 7, 1966, my brother Aaron died in Vietnam. A telegram came early in the morning. I saw it but I can't remember exactly what it said. Something like ... I just recall a few words ... "I am deeply sorry ... inform you ... your son ... killed in action ... ." I was at school. Leah had graduated and was working in a research lab at UCLA. She had her own apartment on Strathmore Street in Westwood.

Mom could hardly get the words out.

"Aaron is dead," she said simply. "Our darling Aaron is gone."

At first, I was too stunned to react. We had always known it could happen, of course, ever since the day he was drafted, but the reality of the situation took time to penetrate. They say that when people receive devastating news, they sometimes deny it. But it never occurred to me to doubt Mom's words. It never occurred to me that there might be some mistake. I knew the instant she said it that it was true. Our darling Aaron was gone.

My whole body began to tremble and finally, I started to sob. I didn't ask questions except whether or not she had called Leah.

"Yes, I called her."

There was nothing more to ask. The details didn't matter.

I could feel my mother's pain over the phone. It was like a heavy, dull pressure right below the breastbone. I wanted to say something to ease her suffering, but what can you say to a mother whose son has just died?

I called a taxi and went home. Leah was already there.

Mom had been crazy, she said. Mom had called Jerry, my brother's ex-roommate, and demanded to talk to Aaron. When Jerry told her that Aaron hadn't lived in the apartment for nearly two years, she had insulted him. She had called him a liar and a mean *ganev* who was trying to keep her away from her son. But now she was calm.

We sat around the kitchen table, Leah, Gail, Mom and I, too excruciated, too dazed even to speak.

After a while, we got up. We cried for hours, each of us alone, in our separate corners, our heads in our hands, our faces pressed against the wall.

The afternoon came. Gail called Dr. Pinkus. Normally he did not make house calls, but this time he came. He gave Mom some pills and Dad a shot to make him sleep. Then he sat back down at the table and drank a cup of coffee with us. He was from the old school of family doctors. He had delivered Aaron.

Gail went across the street to tell Mrs. Sanchez, but Mrs. Sanchez already knew. She had been taking out the garbage when Leah arrived in a taxi, and she was looking out the window when I arrived about fifty minutes later, my face tight and wet. It was an odd hour to be coming home. Mrs. Sanchez knew that something was terribly wrong.

When Gail came back, we were still sitting around the table at which we had talked, laughed, and argued so many times, and at which we had eaten so many nourishing meals—so many pot roasts, so many stuffed cabbages. Mom stared into space, gripping a soaking Kleenex. Sometimes she tore at it, as if trying to tear away Aaron's death.

My own pain was tangible, physical. At first, I felt as though an awl had pierced my stomach, twisting, gutting me alive. Then came the tiny crab claws inside my chest that pinched and grabbed, impeding the flow of air into my lungs. My jaw hurt. My knees hurt. My ankles and arms hurt. I ripped a sleeve, performing unconsciously an ancient Jewish mourning rite that at that time I had never even heard of.

Dad slept a sedative-induced sleep. We knew he would never awaken to be the same father we had known.

The doorbell rang. I was the only one who heard it, and I went to answer.

It was Mrs. Sanchez. She wore a drab blue housedress and no make-up. Her eyes were red and her eyelids raw. Under one arm, she carried a box. With her free arm, she squeezed my shoulders, but said nothing. She had never been in our home before.

Mrs. Sanchez followed me into the kitchen. She put the box down on the table in front of my mother, then opened it for her to see. It was a *kuchen*.

"I bought it from Katz," she said softly. "His wife made it."

Mom looked up at Mrs. Sanchez. At first, she seemed not to understand. But then, a tiny smile of gratitude parted her lips. Leah made room at the kitchen table for Mrs. Sanchez, who sat down next to my mother. Neither woman spoke, but Mom opened her hand, and Mrs. Sanchez took it in her own. After a while, Leah went to lie down, and Gail and I went outside to sit in the garden. The temperature had fallen and the dusk was crisp and fresh. But Mrs. Sanchez and my mother stayed in the kitchen, holding hands and weeping together, for a for a long, long time.

Children

Khaled Al-Maqtari

This is a photograph of a central camp school for Yemeni refugees in Habibti, the Obock governorate, Djibouti. The school is built out of tents. There are no chairs in the classroom, and so the students have to sit on the ground. However, the day this photograph was taken, the refugees went around the camp to claim school dues and other items needed for school, and they returned with chairs. The children were very happy to be able to sit at their desks.

Miss Me Forever

Eugene Garcia-Cross

TULSI IS DREAMING OF oceans when he hears the explosion, a thundering boom that rattles the casement windows of his grandfather's apartment. For a moment he is back in Nepal, in Camp Goldhap, the bamboo walls of his sister's hut casting a ladder of light across the packed earth floor. When he opens his eyes he sees his grandfather at the front door, waving the broom he uses to clean the stoop.

"Poor boys," he yells through the screen. "Poor boys."

It is the night before Halloween, Tulsi's first holiday in the United States. It is a festival he does not yet completely understand. From what he has gathered, it involves human skeletons, candy, and the decoration of giant gourds which are then blown up by the neighborhood boys for sport. Twice this week, Tulsi has heard the explosions and peered out the window to view the orange carnage in the street. Once, while dozing on the pullout that serves as his bed, he was awakened by the splatter of an egg against the window. Tulsi does not like Halloween and will be happy when it has passed.

Tulsi hurries across the apartment, his sandals slapping the ceramic tiles. He steps behind his grandfather and takes the broom from his hands. A piece of stringy pulp sticks in the screen.

"Bad boys, *Hajurba*," Tulsi says as he places his hands on his grandfather's bony shoulders and guides him to his chair. "Here, they are named bad boys."

"Poor in spirit," his grandfather says. He lowers his wiry frame into the tattered La-Z-Boy and with a sudden yank lifts his bare feet into the air. Their soles are the deep red-brown of mahogany and just as hard. "You must not be like them," he says closing his eyes. "You are Nepali. Always remember this."

Tulsi hears the boys laughing, their expensive sneakers pounding the sidewalk as they run away and he thinks, it is impossible not to remember.

Tulsi arrived in the United States a month and a half ago, on an afternoon so impossibly damp and gray, he wondered if he'd landed on the underside of the world. Three days after leaving the transit center in

Katmandu, sleeping on planes and buses and in airport terminals, Tulsi picked his bag off a rotating conveyor belt that slid past his feet like a long steel snake. Outside the airport a husky man with spiked blond hair held a cardboard sign that read Tulsa. A black headset hung from one ear, and he appeared to be talking to himself. When he saw Tulsi staring at the sign, he touched something on the cellular phone attached to his belt and extended his hand. He pulled Tulsi into a half-embrace until their shoulders met.

"You've come a long way, brother," he said, "but your journey is only beginning." Tulsi was not quite sure what the man meant. He was clean-shaven with features like a baby's, soft and rounded. His chin protruded only slightly further than the roll of fat at his neck. He took Tulsi's bag and introduced himself as Pastor Ken, a youth pastor and volunteer for the International Institute. "Call me PK," he said, "that's my nickname. Do you have nicknames in Nepal? We'll get you one pronto," he said and smiled.

On the ride to Tulsi's grandfather's apartment the man spoke endlessly, describing the high school where Tulsi would begin as a fresh-man, the area of town where Tulsi's grandfather now lived, the amount of rain they'd had this summer, and a list of other topics Tulsi only partly understood. Tulsi kept his eyes trained on the world unfolding around him. Four-lane highways divided by concrete slabs, rows of brick factories and warehouses that seemed completely empty, vehicles the size of boats with wheels that spun even when they stood still. He wished his sister, Susmita, were with him. She would be able to explain this place, help him understand. She had remained in Goldhap, teaching at the one-room school where Tulsi himself had been a student. That spring she had married another teacher, a kind man named Purna who was so quiet you had to lean toward him when he spoke, as though his voice held magnetic properties. Tulsi had lived with them until his grandfather was settled in Pennsylvania, a place Tulsi's friends had assured him was governed by vampires. Purna's family would be relocated as well, and once they were, Susmita would travel with them as was their custom. Their new home could be anywhere: Canada, Australia, New Zealand. Tulsi knew it might be months before he heard from her, years before he saw her. He knew he might never see her again.

★ ★ ★

The Tuesday after Halloween, Tulsi takes the bus to Pastor Ken's church, a huge white building with a giant cross on the side and the biggest parking lot he's ever seen. Inside there is a chapel, a gymnasium, a full kitchen, a nursery, and a dozen classrooms. By the time Tulsi finds the one where the ESL class is being held, many of the students are already seated with notebooks spread open before them. Most are dressed in jeans and sweatshirts. Tulsi was unsure what to wear for a class held in a church, and so he has on khakis, beige socks beneath his leather sandals, a white dress shirt, and a tie his grandfather bought him. The tie is pale blue. Stitched onto the front is a giant whale swimming vertically toward Tulsi's face, mouth spread open as though it means to devour him. Pastor Ken spots Tulsi from across the room and jogs over.

"Oklahoma," he says, placing a meaty hand on Tulsi's shoulder. "We'll call you Oklahoma. You know, because I thought your name was Tulsa, but it's not." Tulsi nods uncertainly. While they're speaking, a slender woman in jeans and a T-shirt appears. Tulsi is suddenly very aware of the whale on his tie and crosses his arms over his chest to hide it.

"You must be Tulsi," the woman says. She has the blondest hair he has ever seen. Her eyes are the color of copper. "I'm Abigail, Pastor Ken's wife. I'm here to help out as a conversation partner." Tulsi shakes her hand while keeping one arm crossed over his chest.

"How's Oklahoma?" Pastor Ken asks his wife, wrapping an arm around her waist. "We're trying to figure out a nickname."

Abigail smiles politely as though she's meeting the man standing beside her for the first time. "A bit long. Nicknames are supposed to be easy."

"It's because I thought his name was Tulsa."

Abigail pats her husband's hand where it holds her. "We'll give it some thought," she says.

Pastor Ken opens the ESL class with a prayer. Through a sort of miming routine he instructs everyone on the correct posture: hands clasped, heads bent, eyes closed. Partway through, Tulsi peaks around the classroom. The other students have followed Pastor Ken's instructions with the sort of fervor they all feel is necessary to fit in. Their hands are folded and outstretched before them. Their heads appear glued to their desks. Pastor Ken's eyes are squeezed shut and a strained expression covers his face as though he is lifting a heavy object. He is saying something about trials and sacrifice. Across the room Tulsi sees Abigail watching her husband, a serious look on her face. She is the only one besides himself who does not have their eyes shut. Before Tulsi can put his head back down, Abigail turns and locks eyes with him. For a moment he worries he's in trouble, but then, Abigail smiles.

The class is taught by Mr. Malak, a local professor who is also a member of the church. A tall man with a long gray ponytail, he conjugates verbs on a dry-erase board and makes jokes Tulsi does not understand. The Asian man next to him fills his notebook with furious scribbles even when the professor is not speaking. Tulsi has not brought a notebook, and instead repeats in his mind over and over what Mr. Malak has listed on the board. I am being. I have been. I will be.

★ ★ ★

While he waits at the bus stop, Tulsi leafs through the free Bible each student received after class. He can hardly believe how thin the pages are, like the wings of an insect. Across the road a construction crew is busy digging a trench. As he watches, a yellow car shaped like a helmet pulls near to where he waits. Abigail is driving and waves him over.

"Ken meets with the youth group on Tuesday nights, but I'm headed home. Need a ride?" The air smells of burning leaves and diesel fuel. Across the street a dump truck beeps as it backs up. Abigail reaches over and pushes open the passenger door. "Come on," she says, glancing at his sandals, "your feet must be freezing."

The radio is playing a hymn and for the first few minutes, they listen silently. The sky is a metallic blue with dark clouds that crop up like distant mountains. Tulsi wants to make conversation, but it is hard to think of something to say. Before he can, Abigail says, "I like your tie." Tulsi had momentarily forgotten about the stupid whale tie and looks down to find it clearly visible between the nylon straps of his seatbelt. He cannot imagine why, out of all the ties in their new country, his grandfather chose this one. He almost didn't wear it, but there was his grandfather, smiling his partially-toothless-smile, holding the tie out in both hands like an offering. Tulsi does not think Abigail is being sarcastic though sarcasm is something he has trouble detecting, especially female sarcasm, which is somehow more subtle.

"My grandfather buys it for me," he finally says. Abigail nods as though she knew this was the case.

"Well it's very nice," she says. "It reminds me of the story of Jonah."

"I am not familiar," Tulsi says, surprised to hear himself do so. Normally when he doesn't know what people are talking about he smiles, like at school when the boys in his class argue the finer points of Ultimate Fighting, referencing things like cage matches and grappling, submission holds and fish-hooking, razor-elbows and Brazilian Jiu-Jitsu. Tulsi wants to argue with them, wants to say he's seen some of the fights on late-night cable TV, but joining in their conversation is like jumping on a moving train. Instead he remains silent, listens to their words as they rumble past.

"Jonah and the whale," Abigail says. She reaches over and touches the Bible in Tulsi's lap. "It's in there."

"I am looking before," he says, "very small print." He makes a gesture with his thumb and forefinger like he's crushing a bug, and instantly feels stupid. "It's surprising to me. Everything else in the United States is very big." Abigail laughs a deep laugh.

"I guess that's true," she says, and then her face goes suddenly serious. "It must be a lot different here than in the camps. Do you miss Nepal?"

They are heading north along Peach Street. Below them Lake Erie makes a second, bluer horizon beneath the sky. Tulsi wants to explain the situation as best he can, wants to tell her how the Bhutanese government kicked out all the ethnic Nepalese long before he was born, how the refugee camp was the only home he ever knew. When he was still a baby his mother died from infection, and then his father left. He wants to tell Abigail how his grandfather raised him and how Susmita has another family now, but he only has his grandfather who is getting older and older, dark spots appearing on his skin like the water-stains on the ceiling of their apartment. He wants to tell her how his grandfather works the overnight shift at the juice plant, how tired he looks when he gets home, but how he still waits until Tulsi has finished his breakfast and left for school before he'll sleep. Tulsi wants Abigail to know he'll never be able to repay his grandfather for this. Abigail's car rocks over a pothole. In the distance the faint outline of the moon sits atop a ribbon of clouds. Somewhere on the other side of the world, Tulsi thinks, Susmita is sleeping, her shiny-black hair covering her pillow like spilled ink.

"Some things I miss," he says.

That night Tulsi lies awake on the pullout. His grandfather was already gone when Abigail dropped him off, and the apartment feels even emptier than it normally does. A streetlight shines through the yellowed blinds, throwing stripes across the bare walls. Somewhere a siren blares, and a few blocks up, a freighter rumbles along the tracks above 14th Street. Before he shut off the light, Tulsi read the story of Jonah, how he disobeyed God and ran away from him, how the ship he escaped on was struck by a terrible storm. He read how, after casting lots to see who brought this misfortune upon them, Jonah asked to be thrown overboard into the angry sea. Lying on the mattress, Tulsi imagines himself sinking slowly through dark water, his limbs weightless. He imagines a whale, as big as a mountain, swallowing him whole, the great rush as he's sucked into the belly of the beast. He closes his eyes sealing in the darkness of that place, feels the creature descending, swimming through deep oceans, until after three days it spews him onto a distant shore, far from the land he calls home.

★ ★ ★

Wednesday is the first day of Tihar, and Mr. and Mrs. Bhandari, an elderly Bhutanese couple recently resettled nearby, come over to celebrate. Together they light small clay lamps and pray that good will always triumph over evil. Mrs. Bhandari is kind and smiles at Tulsi, her face so full of wrinkles her features seem lost between them. Her husband ignores Tulsi altogether. He speaks to his grandfather about America as though it is another planet.

"I am not liking it here," he says. "This place is not good for Bhutanese people. It is making them forget our home country and our values." He glances in Tulsi's direction. "Especially young Bhutanese," he adds. "I try not to leave my home, ever. This is my first exit since Monday when we were required to meet with the worker from the resettlement committee." They are sitting at the kitchen table. It is covered with half-empty dishes, a plate heaped with roti, a pot of curried vegetables, and another of spicy dal, bowls of fermented pickles and chutney, and sweets made of almonds, pistachios, and coconut. Tulsi can still taste the burn of the chutney and wets his lips to reignite it. At school they serve mashed potatoes, lukewarm spaghetti, chopped steak in thick brown gravy, food so bland Tulsi eats it only to keep from fainting.

"And if there was a fire?" Tulsi's grandfather asks Mr. Bhandari. "Would you leave then?" He nudges Tulsi below the table with his knee. Tulsi hides a smile, grateful to be the grandson of this man and not the one across the table. Mr. Bhandari considers the question seriously.

"Yes," he finally says, "if there were a fire, then I would leave."

Sunday is Bhai Tika, the final day of the festival. It is the day sisters bless their brothers and pray for their well-being. Every year, for as long as his memory permits, Tulsi recalls Susmita drawing a tika of rice paste on his forehead, Tulsi touching her feet as she prayed that he would live a long and happy life, free from the evils of this world. The night before, Tulsi slept with the phone cradled on his chest. All day he waits for the phone to ring, waits to hear his sister's voice as she asks these things for him once again. But the day drops from beneath him like a trapdoor, and his grandfather leaves for work and the phone does not ring. Tulsi sits in the empty apartment and wonders who will bless him now.

* * *

The next Tuesday Tulsi is the first to arrive at the ESL class. He is wearing a hooded sweatshirt and jeans. He brings a notebook, half a dozen pens, a bottle of water, and a PowerBar. He finds a seat near the front of the class and arranges these items at even intervals before him like a shrine. He focuses on them as the other students trickle in. When Pastor Ken says the opening prayer, Tulsi keeps his forehead pressed against the cool plastic of his desk. Tulsi listens to Mr. Malak intently as though he were offering the key to happiness, for in a way, Tulsi thinks, he is. Twenty minutes into the class, Abigail arrives and takes the open seat beside him. Tulsi smiles at her. She has brought nothing but herself. Taking care to be as quiet as possible, Tulsi tears three sheets from his notebook. He places them on her desk along with a pen.

The instructor makes a list of questions on the board and asks the students to find a conversation partner. They are to take turns interviewing each other.

When Abigail asks him the first question on the list, his favorite food, Tulsi says Philadelphia Cheesesteak. Tulsi has never tried one, but has seen them prepared and eaten on the Food Channel, and Philadelphia is the biggest city in his new state.

"Really?" Abigail asks. "I love those."

"Yes," Tulsi says. "Delicious." All around him he hears his peers struggling with their responses, their thick accents filling the air like a toxic gas. The room feels fuller than usual, cramped as though extra students have been added. Tulsi resents it, this feeling of being crowded. It reminds him of the camps. Above them, the fluorescent lights hum steadily. Tulsi tries to focus on this, whatever will help to drown out the others.

"You know," Abigail says, "for how long you've been here, your English is very strong."

"I studied before leaving," Tulsi says, "at Blooming Lotus English School in our camp. But there we studied British English." A look of recognition lights up Abigail's face. She puts her hands over her heart and pretends to swoon.

"That's it," she says. "I thought I heard a bit of a British accent from you. I adore it. It's so official sounding."

Tulsi's cheeks flush with heat. He picks up a pen, sets it down again. He is flattered and embarrassed. He knows it was meant as a compliment, but still, this is not why he has come to class.

"I want to sound American," Tulsi says, looking away from her when he does.

After class Abigail offers Tulsi a ride home. He thanks her, but says he is planning on making a stop first and doesn't want to delay her.

"I'm in no rush," she says. "Just tell me where we're headed."

It's past eight, but the Wal-Mart lot is filled and they have to park next door at the giant Cineplex built to look like a castle. Inside Wal-Mart, an elderly employee in a cowboy hat and suspenders greets them and pushes a cart toward Tulsi. Fluorescent light reflects off the waxy floor. They pass barrels brimming with discounted DVDs and display cases filled with MP3 players and cameras. There are pyramids of junk food and rack upon rack of clothing. The front left wheel on the cart jiggles incessantly, pulling Tulsi toward aisles he has no wish to enter. There's a vision center, a tire display, a wall of freezers, a lawn and garden department with stone fountains, garden hoses, and bags of soil. Finally they reach the shoe aisle.

Tulsi lives at the corner of 11th and Ash. The kids on his block all wear Nike Air Yeezys and Reebok G-Units. He's taken the bus to the Millcreek Mall and wandered through The Finish Line and Foot Locker, eyeing the wall displays, but all these sneakers are too expensive. Even if he had the money, Tulsi knows he would feel guilty buying a pair. After weeks of saving what his grandfather gives him for lunch, eating nothing but hot dogs, the cheapest thing in his school cafeteria, and drinking only water, he has managed to scrape together $30. Just enough for the newest pair of Champion C9s. He finds them in black then searches for a pair of eights. The closest he can find are nine and a halfs. He slips them on and laces them up.

"Better try them out," Abigail says. At the end of the aisle a mother pushes her cart and yells at her lagging daughter to hurry up. Once they turn the corner and disappear, Tulsi and Abigail are the only two around. Tulsi drops into a sprinter's stance and takes off, running up and down the aisle while Abigail watches and laughs her deep laugh. The sneakers feel like they're going to slip off at any moment, but Tulsi figures he can double up on socks. Better too big than too small. He can grow into them. Abigail leans over the edge of the empty cart applauding.

"Well?" she asks. "How do they feel?"

"Perfect," Tulsi says. He places them back in their box exactly as he found them and puts it in the cart.

In the checkout line Tulsi recognizes another student from the ESL class, a Middle Eastern man named Aban. He is holding a giant package of diapers, and when he sees Abigail and Tulsi, he steps out of line and walks back to them.

"Hello, friends," he says smiling. He is wearing a faded turtleneck beneath his coat, the collar frayed by his thick beard. "A good class tonight." He hefts the package of diapers. "I buy for my baby. Only three weeks old."

Abigail smiles politely and offers a quiet, "Congratulations."

"It is wonderful surprise for me." He looks at Tulsi and asks, "You are student?" It is almost their turn at the register and people are already waiting. Tulsi wishes Aban would not have seen them.

"Yes," he says, inching the cart forward, "at East High School."

"Excellent. Maybe you become doctor, or minister like PK." Aban's brow wrinkles, and for a moment he looks as though he might cry. He turns to Abigail and says, "Your husband is wonderful man."

Abigail nods. "He's very fond of you as well." Her voice sounds flat, distant. Tulsi thinks she's acting strangely and wonders if it's because they have been seen together in public, if this is somehow improper. Aban's face lights up. He clutches the diapers to his chest and nods toward them.

"You have?" he asks. "Baby with PK?" The cashier is waiting for them to step up. Tulsi can feel the eyes of the other people in line. Impatience, he has learned, is something of a birthright in his new home. Abigail is silent. She reaches out and taps her fingers against the handle of the cart, as though checking for stability. She shakes her head.

"No," she says.

★ ★ ★

The car ride home is silent. Abigail grips the wheel like it's something alive she is trying to subdue. Tulsi holds the shoebox in his lap. The clerk did not offer him a bag. He listens to the wind as it sails over the hood. The road they are on cuts through a rising valley Tulsi has never seen before. They might be headed downtown where he lives, but he can't be certain. He wants to check with Abigail, but something tells him he should keep quiet. A line of clouds floats past a bone-white moon, and in the distance, below the rise of the road, Tulsi spots the oily black surface of a pond. Abigail is staring straight ahead and suddenly she says, "Why did he have to ask that?" Her voice sounds different and Tulsi feels the tiny hairs on the back of his neck prickle. A home for the elderly sits in a clearing above the road. It is built low and wide, and some of the windows are lit up like portholes on a ship. "What kind of a question is that?" Abigail says.

Tulsi is unsure what to say, and so he says nothing. Abigail is still not looking at him, and he senses that she does not expect him to answer. The road descends into the valley where the shadows of trees have darkened the asphalt, and for a moment Tulsi feels the sensation of being submerged.

Abigail cranks down her window, and the car floods with a sudden rush of freezing air, the sound it makes deafening. Tulsi keeps his head lowered, his eyes trained on the lettering of the box, which seems even more unfamiliar to him now. After a moment Abigail turns to him, surprised, it seems, that he is sitting beside her.

"I'm sorry," she says. "It's been a long day, a long couple of days, and I'm very tired."

Tulsi nods. Slowly he is beginning to understand. Abigail offered him a kindness, and he made a mistake. He took too long at the store, and now it is late.

"I'm sorry for this," he says, patting the box. "It is dark out, and I am keeping you."

"No," Abigail says. "That's not it at all. I'm glad you found your shoes. I'm glad you like them." She pats his hand, and instantly Tulsi forgets the guilt he was just feeling. Abigail rolls her window back up and adjusts the heater so that it blows a steady stream of warm air. A lone strand of hair falls over her forehead. Tulsi watches as she blows upward, setting it in motion.

"If you're happy I am too," she says. She turns to him and smiles, holds his eyes steady with hers. "You're happy, aren't you?"

Tulsi pulls the shoebox closer, feels the warm air from the heater wash over him. Abigail is driving him home, and he trusts she knows the way. "Yes," he tells her. "I am happy."

★ ★ ★

A few days later Tulsi sees snow for the first time. Fat flakes descend from bulging clouds and cover cars and benches, the naked branches of trees. For three days it does nothing but snow, and for three days Tulsi watches. Giant yellow plows fight through the drifts, forming banks along the sides of roads, building tiny mountains at the edges of parking lots. Tulsi is afraid to go outside, afraid to touch it. The temperature continues to drop, and the snow glazes over with a thin coat of ice that sparkles like crushed glass. At night his grandfather wraps shopping bags over his socks and sandals and ties them with twine. Tulsi watches him slip and stumble along the sidewalk on his way to work. Tulsi tells his grandfather he is sick and cannot attend school. Tuesday comes, and he skips the ESL class. He stays inside the apartment all day wrapped in a thick shawl Susmita made for him before he left. When he first arrived, it smelled like her, like cardamom and lavender, but now when Tulsi holds the shawl to his face and inhales, he smells only the cold. He wonders if Purna's family has been issued their resettlement orders, if Susmita has left Nepal. He wonders if it is snowing where she is.

★ ★ ★

On Thursday there is a knock at the door. Tulsi walks across the room, the shawl draped over his shoulders like a cape. He opens to find Abigail standing in the snow. She is wearing a bright red winter coat, a yellow scarf, and a green knit cap. She reminds Tulsi of a rainbow. He wants to say so, but instead invites her in.

"You weren't in class the other night," she says. "I was worried." She is holding a large brown package tied with string. "Are you sick?"

Tulsi shrugs his shoulders and the shawl slips from one, dangles to the floor.

"It's beautiful," Abigail says, pointing at it.

"My sister made it for me," he says, surprised to hear the words come out of his mouth. This is the first time since arriving that he's spoken of Susmita to anyone but his grandfather.

Abigail looks intrigued. "I didn't know you had a sister," she says. "What's her name?"

"Susmita," he says. "I lived with her and her husband before I came here."

"You must miss her very much," Abigail says. Tulsi lifts the shawl from the floor and begins to fold it.

"She wanted me to come here," he says, "to live with our *Hajurba*." Tulsi points toward the bedroom. "He is asleep." Lately his grandfather has been picking up extra shifts, volunteering to fill in when other employees request off for the holidays. He arrives home exhausted, too tired even to eat.

"I'm sure she thought it was for the best," Abigail says. Tulsi nods. He remembers how in the weeks leading up to his departure, Susmita would only speak with him in English. She wanted him to be prepared, to be ready for his new home. If he tried to engage her in Nepali, she would cover her ears and hum. He remembers his frustration, trying to communicate at such an important time in a language not his own.

"I brought this for you," Abigail says, handing him the package. Tulsi accepts it hesitantly.

They sit across from each other at the kitchen table. Tulsi unties the string taking care not to rip the brown wrapping paper. Inside is a navy blue winter coat and matching hat. Both feature the trademark Nike Swish logo in stark white. Tulsi runs his fingertips over the cool nylon.

"I wasn't sure if you had any winter clothes," Abigail says and smiles. "I know the weather here isn't quite the same."

Tulsi touches the smooth fabric once more then folds the wrapping paper over it. "I am sorry. I cannot accept," he says and slides the package across the table.

Abigail looks confused. "You don't like it?" she asks.

"I like it very much, but I cannot repay you."

"You don't have to," Abigail says and pushes the package back toward Tulsi. "It's a gift." She smiles and motions toward it. "Take it. It's nothing."

Tulsi sits quietly for a moment. He knows he shouldn't but finally he lifts the package and holds it to his chest. "It is something," he says.

★ ★ ★

Outside it is still snowing. The sidewalks have not been shoveled and so they walk along the icy street, snow crunching below Tulsi's C9s. He is wearing his new coat and hat. The air is crisp against his skin. He feels better than he has in days. Abigail asks him why he skipped the ESL class, and he tells her.

"This," he says pointing at the bank that comes up to his waist. "It is something new to me."

Abigail laughs. "You'll have to get used to it living here," she says. "Besides, it's not so bad." She kicks at a mound of powder near her foot, and Tulsi watches it explode in the air like smoke. The sun shines above the apartment complexes to the west and makes the snow glimmer. Tulsi leans down and scoops up a small handful. It looks like a mound of cotton, wet and cold in his bare palm. Abigail scoops some up as well then crunches it in both hands. "Perfect for snowballs," she says. She winds up and tosses it toward a stop sign but misses to the right.

Tulsi makes his own and hits the sign above the p.

"Nice shot," she says. The two of them stand there tossing snowballs, seeing who can hit closest to the middle of the sign. The light begins to fail, and the street lights switch on, and after a while Abigail says she has to go. Tulsi thanks her for the coat and hat and watches her walk back to her car. He waves as she drives by. For a long time he stays there, pitching snowballs at the sign until the fingers of his throwing hand go numb.

★ ★ ★

The Tuesday before Thanksgiving arrives and in lieu of a lesson, the ESL class has a party in the church gymnasium. Mr. Malak has asked the students to bring a dish native to their home country. He has told them this is called a "Potluck." Tulsi arrives late wearing his C9s and his Nike coat and hat. He is carrying a bag of Doritos he bought at the corner store near the bus stop. The others have all dressed up. The men wear threadbare sports coats from Goodwill. Their slacks are mismatched and too short, revealing white tube socks and second-hand dress shoes. Some of the women sport Saris while others have on faded dresses. Everyone is smiling and laughing, holding plates of food and glasses of punch, but somehow, all of it strikes Tulsi as sad. He walks directly to the long folding table to set down his chips. He scans the gym for Abigail, but sees no sign of her or PK. Mr. Malak is standing at the far end of the basketball court talking to Aban. Tulsi walks over and interrupts them.

"Is Abigail been here?" he asks. Mr. Malak looks down and smiles.

"Has Abigail been here," he says. Tulsi repeats him and he nods approvingly the way he does during class. "They were here earlier, but only to say goodbye."

"Goodbye?" Tulsi asks. Across the gym, two Sudanese women from class break into song. They sway side by side, arms around each other's waists. Tulsi watches momentarily and then says again, "Goodbye?"

"PK has been offered the senior pastor position at another church. Unfortunately, he and Abigail will be leaving us soon."

"PK was very excited," Aban says while looking at Mr. Malak.

"Yes, he was, Aban. Nice job."

"I am confused," Tulsi manages to say. His heart is beating fast as though he's just finished running. His head is suddenly dizzy, his legs weak. "How can this be so?"

"We hate to see PK and Abigail go, but the Lord has called them elsewhere. It's His will."

Tulsi feels a rush of panic, the same way he felt as he climbed into the van that took him from Goldhap, everything he owned packed into a cloth duffel bag in his lap. He remembers Susmita calling his name, waving to him as the van pulled away until she was nothing more than a faceless onlooker in the crowd. Sometimes, when he tries to think of her now, he cannot picture her face.

"It's bittersweet," Mr. Malak says. "Do you know that word? Bittersweet?" Tulsi shakes his head.

"It's something good that also makes you sad. Do you understand?"

"No." Tulsi says and turns to go.

At the information booth in the lobby Tulsi finds a church directory. The first few pages contain pictures of the ministry staff with their families, smiling couples flanked by children in tiny suits and ruffled dresses, God's workers in miniature. On the last page are PK and Abigail. PK's hair looks extra spiky, his doughy face stretched into a smile. He is standing behind a seated Abigail, his big hands resting on her shoulders. Abigail is wearing a white dress with black flowers on it. She is beaming, her hands folded in her lap. Above them her dress swells at the stomach, a prominent bump that cannot be mistaken. Tulsi runs his fingers over the picture, the page glossy and cool. Finally, he thinks, he is beginning to understand.

Beneath the picture is a phone number and address. Tulsi writes them down on a piece of church stationery and leaves.

The first bus driver tells him to wait for the Number 17 and get off at the third stop. When it arrives, Tulsi takes a seat alone in back. It's only five o'clock, and already the light is failing. A thin haze of violet floats above a line of trees in the distance. The air looks smoky, and the drive-ways and lawns on either side are covered in white. By the time Tulsi gets off the bus it is full dark and beginning to snow. He walks east until he reaches Costa Drive. Most of the houses are lit up. Tulsi reads the numbers on the mailboxes until he finds 112. It's a tiny two-story home with a shoveled stone walkway and lavender window boxes. Abigail's car sits in the driveway covered in a shell of snow. The house is set back from the road. Tulsi wants to go right up and knock on the door, but senses the impropriety in this. He was not invited. He has never vis-ited their home. He worries how he will answer if PK opens the door, what he will say if asked how he's found their address. Instead, Tulsi cuts through an adjacent yard, taking care to stay close to a row of evergreens that runs parallel to a darkened garage. His sneakers crunch through the icy snow. Somewhere nearby a dog barks. Tulsi ducks against the hedges and waits for it to quiet. He jams his bare hands deep into the pockets of his coat. His feet are freezing, and as he waits snow begins to cover his sleeves. He can feel the flakes settling in his collar. He tries to keep from shivering, but it's hard. He's never felt so cold in his life.

When the barking stops he continues to move, staying low to the ground. After what seems like forever he reaches the end of the hedges and cuts through an opening into PK and Abigail's backyard. A clean sheet of snow covers the frozen grass. Unlike some of the other yards on the street, theirs is empty. No grill, no bird feeder, no swing set. Behind a sliding glass door, the dining room is lit up. The light casts a bluish sheen over the snow before dying into darkness. Abigail and PK sit side by side at the table, their hands clasped together, their eyes closed. They are facing him and from where he stands, Tulsi can see PK's lips mov-ing, the urgency with which he speaks. His face looks the way it does when he prays in class, full of pain and wonder. Abigail's face is blank, her mouth set in a rigid line. After a while PK stops speaking and leans against Abigail until their cheeks touch. He kisses her on the temple, stands, and leaves the room. Tulsi looks up and follows the snowflakes as high as he can before they disappear in the dark. It isn't that far. A wind comes rushing down the yard and cuts straight through his coat chilling his skin. He wants to step closer, wants to stand where the light touches the snow. He takes a step, then another. Abigail has her elbows on the table and is holding her head as if it weighs a thousand pounds. Her shoulders heave, but Tulsi can't tell if she is crying or coughing. He wants to know. He takes another step, and when he does a motion light clicks on bathing the yard in light. Abigail looks up and for a moment, Tulsi stands perfectly still, unable to breathe. Abigail tilts her head from side to side, rushes to the window and cups her hands to the sides of her face. Tulsi is unsure if she can see him. She raises her hand and bangs her knuckles against the glass as though to frighten an animal. Tulsi hears the dog barking again, this time closer. Another light goes on in a neighboring yard. Tulsi turns and runs.

He goes back the way he came, his feet crashing through the crusty snow. When he reaches the front of the house, he realizes he's lost one of his sneakers. He keeps running down the sidewalk, his socked foot pounding against the cold and wet concrete. Behind him there are headlights. He cuts through a yard, and then across the road into a stand of woods. He stumbles over snow-covered underbrush, his hands held out before him like a blind man. Branches whip at his face. A car door slams. He stops, falls to the earth and crawls behind a nearby tree, sits with his back against it. He cannot be sure but he thinks he has made it deep into the woods, too deep to be seen from the road. For a moment there is nothing. And then there is Abigail.

"Tulsi," she yells. Her voice sounds far away. "Tulsi, I know it's you. I saw you in the yard." Tulsi doesn't move. He cannot feel his fingers. His sock is soaked through, and his foot throbs. His sneaker is gone.

"Listen," Abigail says, "you don't have to come out, but just listen." Tulsi leans back hard, feels the bark press pain into his spine. He does not want to listen. He does not want to hear a word. He wants to cover his ears, jam pinecones in them, scream until his lungs burn and set fire to his frozen body. He rests his chin against his sternum, and then, with as much strength as he can manage, slams his head backward against the trunk. He does this again, keeps his eyes open so that the world jars as though trying to right itself. Susmita is gone forever. Her children will never know him. His grandfather will work himself to death in this cold place where no one waits for anything. Abigail is leaving.

"I know you're upset," she says, "that you think you're being abandoned. I've felt that way too."

Nearby a branch cracks and falls under the weight of the wet snow. Something warm trickles down the back of his neck and soaks into his shirt. He thinks about running further into the woods until he reaches the darkest part. He imagines living in the hollowed out center of a giant tree, surviving on nuts and berries, drinking water from a clear stream, never again speaking to another living soul. It is a crazy, childish fantasy. But people have done things like this. He stays still and holds his breath. His head is spinning, white dots float near the edge of his vision. Abigail has left the headlights on, and thin cuts shine through the branches. He remembers Susmita's hut, the way the morning light filtered through the bamboo slats. He remembers waking late, the rib work of wood beams above him, Purna and his sister already gone for the day. He remembers dressing in the stifling heat while dust particles fell through the hazy light, pulling on his sandals before rushing outside to find his friends.

The morning he left Camp Goldhap he wanted so badly to speak to Susmita in Nepali, but even then she insisted he use English, told him it was more important than ever. He remembers standing in line beneath the scorching sun, UN volunteers helping the elderly and very young as they boarded the vans that would take them away. Soon it would be his turn. Soon he would be gone. What he wanted to tell Susmita was to never forget him, to always remember him, her brother. He recalls the frustration he felt at trying to translate the words in his head. When it was his turn to climb aboard the van, Susmita drew him close and held him like he was all she had in the world. When she released him he looked up at her and said, "Miss me forever." They were the last words he spoke to her.

Tulsi knows now there is a difference. He understands it is a subtle difference, but that it still exists. He would never have wished Susmita a fraction of the sadness he's felt since leaving. He only wanted to not be forgotten.

A strong wind rushes through the trees. Tulsi's entire body aches, stung by the cold. Slowly, he raises himself to his feet in the darkness. Abigail is calling him and he turns toward the direction of her voice. He moves carefully, feeling for branches with outstretched hands, lifting his feet high to keep from tripping. He knows now how to speak the words he could not say to Susmita. Knows the proper way to say goodbye.

That's Not Nostalgia

Olga Livshin

LATTAKIA, SYRIA – PHILADELPHIA, USA –

see: flight, exile, nostalgia, in that order.
That face of exile, that patina-coated profile,
ennobled by Ovid, suspiciously granted
to people of your origin, color. Someone
banished you; he will be punished, and soon.
For now, we exiles' great-grandkids let you in,

but why is the face so gay, delicate, yours?
Puffs of ginger fur float around your face.
Your mouth is filled with *kasha varnishkes*
of words—one language, under God, indivisible—
undercooked, while two others taste of kibbeh
and cherries, no matter how much

you try to forget. What if you care most
about your sister's wedding, which you missed,
not having seen your family in years? That's not
nostalgia. And this isn't a face. The ass-crack
of exile, the beak of flight, light turned around
by running webbed feet. Sir, ma'am—dammit,

person—you are supposed to stop running.
You have arrived in exile … Enough. If we stop
calling you our words, we may yet see you
as ambiguous as our own families. See that your
story is to be continued. Distilled, for now,
as wild sadness on your lips,

which shape your own mangled truth:
My sister is named Nareman.
See the picture on my phone? See how she presiding
over the family in her tiara? See her white dress,
that fountain of light? Spills into every corner
of all you can see from here.

This poem first appeared in Olga Livshin's book, *A Life Replaced: Poems with Translations from Anna Akhmatova and Vladimir Gandelsman*, Poets & Traitors, 2019.

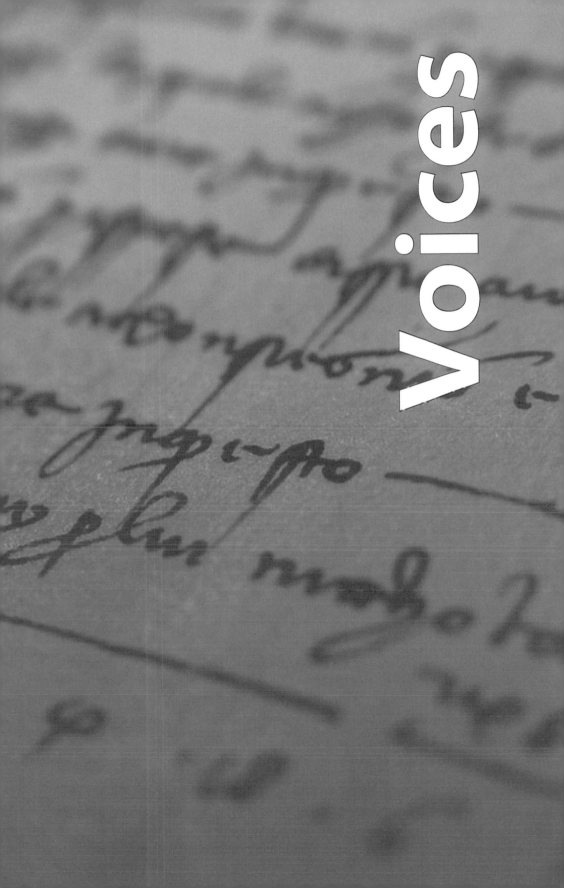

Voices

Elegy for My Mother's Employer

Mihaela Moscaliuc

Exit 172, Garden State Parkway, New Jersey

Why not, she'd snap as she ordered the tiles scrubbed raw
five empty bottles of cleaner lined for inspection
sixty-five pansies planted then replanted closer to the brick border
silver bowls emptied then reloaded with orchid-shaped
no not the lotus-shaped candles.
Why not swill fine cellar wine directly from the bottle
why not waltz while mother cooks onions in the rain
so they won't pollute the inside with their crass smell
why not waltz naked, extoll your small frame
and freckled breasts, why not kick across the floor
each cocktail dress in search of the one
that will outshine the daughter.
Why not, she repeats, like a mantra, *why wouldn't I?*
Six months of this shit's enough, I tell my mother.
I'd heard Romanians treated their own like servants,
harping on how much worse their lives
would be back home, but now the rage
is personal. Pack up, we'll come get you.
Mother assures me she's fine. The woman means
no harm. She's just having a hell of a time
dying in this marmoreal house
in a language that trips the tongue,
so far from the steamy furrows of native ground.

Confiar / Trust

Marjorie Agosín

Confiar que las cosas abandonadas volverán a ser hermosas.
Confiar en el ritmo de los días sin premura.
Confiar en una sonrisa y en el tiempo del azar.
Confiar que cuando acaricias el cabello de un niño,
Se acercan aún más las estrellas …
Te acercas tú más a las estrellas.

Confiar en las palabras que no hablan de la guerra,
Tan solo las que se brindan en el luminoso lenguaje de los días.
Confiar en los inocentes y en los perseguidos.
Dudar de los que levantan la voz y castigan con su severidad.

Confiar en el otoño,
La manifestación de las hojas,
El tiempo de la luz que hechiza.
Confiar en el paso de las estaciones,
Esas horas entre los intervalos de la claridad.

Confiar en la bondad,
En los actos que desafían el odio.
Confiar en los niños que sólo deben jugar.
Confiar en los sentimientos, los buenos deseos …

Confiar que nadie miente frente al amor.
Confiar que no hay traición en el amor,
Tan solo la fluidez de los pequeños desencuentros.
Confiar en las pasiones inocentes,
Las que juegan en la luminosa oscuridad de los días.

Confiar en los maestros, en los médicos y los estudiantes.
Confiar que la voz no se cierra,
Tan solo se abre como un girasol.
Confiar en los ancianos;
Ellos tienen el derecho a contar sobre el pasado.

Confiar en los puentes y no los precipicios.
Confiar en el futuro con la claridad del pasado.
Confiar en el oleaje y en la roca,
En todos los puertos y todas las llegadas.

Confiar en el espacio de la música
Cuando canta y cuando no dice.
Confiar en la solidaridad de los músicos que se acompañan,
En la soledad de los poetas que se acompañan con las palabras.

Confiar en un amor imaginario,
En los que están lejos y de ellos nada sabemos,
Igual confiamos en el misterio de que son buenos.
Confiar en el silencio que tanto nos dice.
Desconfiar del silencio que no dice y es tan solo vacío.

Confiar en una caricia y en una mano,
En una noche de invierno cuando te dan una frazada.
Confiar en los que rescatan,
En los que te ofrecen un techo y un vaso de agua.

Confiar en los cumpleaños,
Nacimientos extraordinarios.
Confiar para poder vivir en el estado de la gracia,
En el espíritu de las cadencias y las intuiciones.

Confiar en ti.

Trust that abandoned things will be beautiful once more.
Trust in the rhythm of unhurried days.
Trust in a smile and in the time of chance.
Trust that when you stroke a child's hair,
The stars come closer still …
You move closer to the stars.

Trust in words that do not speak of war,
Only those that offer the luminous language of everyday.
Trust in the innocent and the persecuted.
Doubt those who raise their voices and punish with their bluster.

Trust in the autumn
With its show of leaves,
The time of bewitching light.
Trust in the passing seasons,
Those hours amid the recesses of understanding.

Trust in goodness,
In acts that thwart hate.
Trust in children who should only be playing.
Trust in feelings, good wishes …

Trust that no one will lie in the face of love.
Trust there is no treachery in love,
Only the impermanence of minor disputes.
Trust in innocent passions
That play in the luminous darkness of days.

Trust in teachers, doctors and students.
Trust that voices do not quiet,
But open like sunflowers.
Trust in the elderly;
They have the right to speak about the past.

Trust in bridges, not precipices.
Trust in the future with the clarity of the past.
Trust In the surf and the rocks,
In every port and every arrival.

Trust in the time of music,
When one sings and does not speak.
Trust in the harmony of musicians who accompany one another,
In the solitude of poets kept company by words.

Trust in an imaginary love,
In those who are far away and out of touch,
As we trust in the mystery of their kindness.
Trust in the silence that tells us so much.
Distrust the silence that is mute and vacant.

Trust in a caress and a helping hand,
In a winter's night when you are given a blanket.
Trust in those who rescue,
In those who offer you shelter and a glass of water.

Trust in birthdays,
Extraordinary births.
Trust in order to live in a state of grace,
In the spirit of cadences and intuition.

Trust in you.

(Translated from Spanish by Alison Ridley.)

Montage: Iran Present Tense

Elizabeth Eslami

O N APRIL 30 IN Tel Aviv, when Israeli Prime Minister Benjamin Netanyahu kicked off his prop-heavy presentation on Iran's "secret atomic archive," he didn't bury the lede. Prior to the shelves of binders or the disks unveiled *Price is Right*-style, Netanyahu began with two words in Times New Roman: Iran lied. No period, as if the past tense weren't really past but a continuation into an uncertain point in the future. No adverb. Iran lied. Then White House Press Secretary Sarah Huckabee Sanders, forming a slightly more complex sentence than Netanyahu's, floated her own version of "Iran Lied": "These facts are consistent with what the United States has long known: Iran has a robust, clandestine nuclear weapons program that it has tried and failed to hide from the world and from its own people." Has or had, now or then? The point was, *is*, that the Iranians are liars.

My father, who emigrated to the United States from Iran, told me when I was a kid that you have to watch Iranians: they lie. About what? About everything, he said. This was during the hostage crisis, back when everyone hated the Iranians, but before McCain sang "Bomb, Bomb Iran" 30 years later and everyone laughed—because they still hated the Iranians. This business about the Iranians being liars didn't make sense to me. When I saw Iranians on television during the Reagan years— burning effigies, shouting Death to America, which I'd learn years later was a mistranslation—the images didn't make me think of lying. The Iranians on television didn't have a hidden agenda. Their agenda was in full view, with a prepositional object: Death to America, or better translated, down with American policies.

Still, the lying Iranians story has persisted. Oliver North, once front and center for Iran-Contra and, for a brief tenure, the president of the NRA, went on Fox News in 2018 to declare, "Never believe an Iranian— because if their lips are moving, they're lying." I heard the story from my cousin in 2010, herself freshly emigrated to the United States, as we drove away from JFK. "You can't trust them. They'll say one thing to your face, another behind your back." She'd been the recipient of the visa lottery, which Trump views like a game show. If my cousin had tried to come eight years later, she'd have run up against the travel ban.

Strangely for my family, the story of Iranian liars was not at all incompatible with the story of Iranians as the kindest people in the world, the latter being my experience. Iranians will invite you to dinner the minute they meet you, send gifts across the world, turquoise and leather and handmade sweaters. My half-American family would reciprocate with Forever 21 shirts made in Taiwan. If I asked someone on either side of the family, American or Iranian, they'd say "Iranians are the most generous people on the planet." But, I'd point out, I thought you told me they were liars. "Yeah, they're that, too."

When Donald Trump decided to pull out of the Iran deal, he carefully distinguished between the Iranian people and the Islamic Republic. He praised the people as part of a "proud nation," gave lip service to them as "an honor to their history," as if the United States never meddled in that history, no mention of Mosaddegh, no mention of decades of sanctions that hurt those very people, shuttered small businesses, drove up the cost of groceries. Obviously there's a distinction to be made between people and policy, just as there are differences between "the mullahs"— which the Trump administration uses as synecdoche for the Islamic Republic—and President Rouhani, between Supreme Leader Khamenei and Rouhani, and certainly between hard-liners and reformers. In recent years, it's hard to imagine a starker contrast than between Rouhani and his predecessor, Mahmoud Ahmadinejad, who famously fulminated outright lies at the UN. Back in Iran, Ahmadinejad was more subdued. A journalist friend who interviewed both Ahmadinejad and Syria's Assad marveled over the differences between the two men. With Assad, you can tell him to his face he's a madman, but he looks calm, educated, well-dressed, like the ophthalmologist he once was. When I think of Ahmadinejad, the journalist said, I see him in his gym socks and a sad windbreaker, a blusterer out of his depth. Ahmadinejad had someone take all of the American journalists to Tehran's shuttered Metropolitan Museum of Art for a private tour. Ahmadinejad wasn't the least bit interested in art. It was a strange tour, full of lies: all the "dirty" paintings were covered up.

My face tells a lie. It says I'm American or I'm Iranian, or something. I don't speak Farsi. Another writer, born in the United States to an American mother and an Iranian father, said, "Yeah, you're like me.

We're not real Iranians." Maybe my last name gives me away, but mostly people assume that I'm *something*, just not Iranian. You say it funny, people tell me. Eee-rahn. But that's how you say it, I protest. Once, in college, I sat next to a guy who wouldn't stop staring at me. After class, the guy announced, "It's your nose. I knew you had to be something." My journalist friend told me that Iran has the most beautiful women in the world. Yeah, I said, and all of them come to America and get nose jobs.

Sometimes, I think Americans' views on Iran are evolving. Where before there was *Not Without My Daughter*, with the lying not-really-Iranian patriarch, Americans now watch Iranian vampire spaghetti Westerns. After his film *The Salesman* won the Academy Award, Asghar Farhadi, protesting Trump's travel ban, declined to attend. "My absence is out of respect for the people of my country ... who have been disrespected by the inhumane law that bans entry of immigrants to the U.S. Dividing the world into the us and our enemies categories creates fear, a deceitful justification for aggression and war." As Trump himself might say, *somebody's* doing the deceiving, and it's not just Iran.

When the United States pulled out of the Iran deal, did we get to call that process "reversing a disastrous deal"? "Shifting strategy"? What if, as former White House negotiator Robert Malley has suggested, pulling out means that "America's word is not going to be as trusted"? Surely that wouldn't make *us* liars. We don't lie; we use alternative facts. There are complex and nuanced reasons for how America will proceed here, right?

On May 8, 2018, Donald Trump, echoing Netanyahu, unveiled his decision, likely made a long time before: "Today, we have definitive proof that this Iranian promise was a lie." Iran lied. Or: Iran lies, for all time. Note that the adverb, today, is at odds with the verb; in fact, nothing was discovered today or yesterday or last month. Does it matter that Mike Pompeo admitted that there was no new intelligence telling us that Iran was no longer compliant with the JCPOA? Does it matter that, according to the *Observer*, Donald Trump wrote this story back in 2017, when his aides hired an Israeli intel firm to dig up dirt on Obama administration officials negotiating the deal, to pave the way for a future when he'd pull out? Has or had, now or then?

When I teach my first-year students creative writing, sometimes they inadvertently switch verb tenses. I teach them to be consistent, that the timeline of a story matters.

I am a liar. I told my grandmother, in Iran, that I'd come to visit her before she died. That I'd leave this America that swallowed her son, that I'd be the one, finally, to return. She kept my photograph on the mantel before she died. I could tell you that people warned me not to go, that I was warned against the complications of dual citizenship, that I could be detained. That's true, just as it's true that I know plenty of people, Iranian and half-Iranian, who have gone to Iran and come back. I could tell you those truths but I'd still be lying, because my grandmother, my relatives, they were all waiting for me, and I didn't go. I didn't know, I *don't* know, who to be, how to be, in this Iran. Present tense.

La Bestia / The Beast

A Visual Investigation of the Journey of Undocumented Unaccompanied Central American Minors Crossing the Mexico–United States Border

Claudia Bernardi

ACCORDING TO THE US Office of Refugee Resettlement, a total of 50,036 unaccompanied undocumented minors were taken into custody after crossing the border in fiscal 2018. Most of the children, 30 percent of them younger than twelve years old, from El Salvador, Guatemala, Honduras, and Mexico, crossed the United States–Mexico border alone, or with adults who were not relatives, often fleeing poverty, corruption, and violence hoping to seek asylum in the United States.

Since 2015, I have been facilitating community-based and collaborative mural projects with undocumented, unaccompanied, Central American migrant minors detained in maximum security prisons in the United States. Although I had worked in art projects in jails before, I wasn't sure what to expect working within the criminal justice system in the United States. The first major difference from other projects that I had facilitated was that the participants were very young, between thirteen and seventeen years of age, both female and male. The average age of everyone I met was fifteen years old. As soon as one of the undocumented incarcerated minors would turn eighteen, he or she, would be transferred to an adult facility.

The young men and women I met in this project were the generation born after the end of the twelve-year long civil war in El Salvador. The conflict expanding from 1980 to 1992 was followed by social, institutional and economic collapse in the postwar period. Manufactured imposed poverty in Central America added to the devastation produced by recent wars. When we embarked in the creation of this mural project using the tactics of art to learn about the personal and communal stories of these children, I did not know that many of them had been victims of human rights violations both in their countries of origin and, sometimes, in the United States.

I initiated this project hoping that the completed collaborative mural, which was painted on canvas and could travel, would be exhibited in art venues as well as in universities and community centers all over the country. This mural would broadcast a current situation that was hidden or incorrectly and insufficiently known by the vast majority of US citizens.

Painting a community-based mural creates an atmosphere of collaboration in which personal recollections expand into collective reminiscence expanding the membrane that isolates people from *"others"* because of prejudice, misassumptions, ignorance, or indifference. A collaborative mural becomes a possible ample geography on which a new reading of identities is being proposed. One of the strategies used to build a collaborative mural resides on sharing personal and collective memories. A memory becomes a drawing and a scene in a mural after the participating group accepts the uniqueness of a personal experience within the vastness of a joined social space. Initial drawings and sketches eventually become the composition of the mural. Memories are a commemoration against forgetting.

As the facilitator of a community-based and collaborative mural I emphasize that all decisions will be taken by consensus, I ask concrete questions that focus on the creative process, avoiding altercation or hostility. Is there any image that does not respond to the initial shared idea? Do the drawings need reconsideration? I recommend considering scale, color, location of the image in the mural.

None of the participants had painted a mural before or had participated in a collaborative art project. Most of them had, however, seen murals in the towns or cities where they were born or while traveling to the United States. Each mural is a book of history without words. What is the story that *you* want to tell? The visual testimony of the undocumented, unaccompanied, Central American minors depicted in vibrant colors and unintimidated lines and shapes, showed their perilous journey crossing from El Salvador, Honduras, Guatemala, and Mexico until they entered the United States and were captured by the US Border Patrol. They rode on the roof of *La Bestia*/The Beast, that endless train that crosses Mexico from Tapachula, Arriaga, or Ixtepec to Ciudad Juárez or Nogales. This was a treacherous ride where people were killed, women were raped, most were robbed, and many would never reach the border. Some people were pushed and had fallen off the train. They were left behind with amputated legs or arms. No one knows how many died on the train tracks. An estimated half a million Central American immigrants annually hop aboard that catastrophic cargo train which runs along multiple lines, transiting the routes of Mexico from south to north.

The participating artists of this project had been desperate when they left their towns and villages. They were willing to walk the map of Central America not knowing, really, how far El Salvador was from Guatemala. They had not learned in El Salvador or Honduras that after Guatemala, they still had to cross Mexico. A Honduran boy who had never gone to school and hardly knew how to write or read, said that it had never occurred to him that he was crossing borders. He could not discern when the countries changed from being one into another. In his memory, all the people he had met in his voyage looked and talked pretty much the same. They were all distressed, hungry, tired, and frightened. Some of them cried inconsolably.

In the mural, the young artists addressed the urgency they had faced which forced them to leave hoping to escape terror and trauma by "going North", an option that they thought might alleviate an unsustainable situation in their homelands. They knew that it was going to be risky to be undocumented in the endless land of the north but, what alternative did they have? There was no work in El Salvador or Guatemala. Honduras had become the most dangerous country in the world. Mexico was a narco-state where the cartels dominated the life and death of everyone.

They had heard about the endless harms that the human cargo suffered on top of *La Bestia*. They had not anticipated, however, that they would become subject to extortion and violence at the hands of organized criminals who would size them at the border demanding money that they could not pay in exchange for the right of crossing. When they could not produce the funds, they were obliged to pay in a different way. Girls and women of all ages became sexual slaves and victims of sex trafficking. Young men were forced to witness hideous crimes, or they were given weapons to become assassins themselves to save their own lives.

The development of community-based and collaborative murals is rooted in the building of *trust* among the participants. In pain, *trust* is lost. People tormented by violence will retain a profound distrust at all times. The creation of a communal mural is an exercise on *trust*-building. Unlike the most traditional model of art education that focuses on individual choices, community-based and collaborative murals depart from the opposite paradigm: the collective effort will define the intention of the art piece. A mural would never remedy the inflicted pain that the young artists had undergone, but the collaborative aspect of painting a mural as a group, effectively, becomes a tool for reconstruction. The mural is an antidote to a persistent sadness and inconceivable solitude. The proposition of community building through the practice of art constitutes not only a new model of art education but a suggestion to consider art as a way in which *ethics*, *aesthetics* and *politics* merge.

This mural created in two integrated panels that culminated in a diptych was the first attempt known in the United States in which art met legal concerns, health, social justice, education, social work, sociology, and anthropology providing to the undocumented, unaccompanied Central American minors a safe visual geography on which to deposit their turbulent and traumatic illegal transit from poverty and violence experienced in their countries to the unknown challenges of being undocumented and now, incarcerated, in the United States. The main character of the mural is the train, *La Bestia*/The Beast, traveling from right to left, from past to present and into the future. The train, which appears rusty and old in the past, becomes lighter and better preserved in the present until it becomes transparent and luminous in the future while it enters a tunnel of faith and hope. The line of the horizon announces a broad distance between the journey The Beast is taking and the expected arrival to a destiny less cruel than the one they had faced. Two erupting volcanoes are messengers of the power stored within the earth. One of those firing mountains is female, *la Volcana*, a source of wisdom and truth. The female fire has the face of an aging woman who has seen everything, has endured the unthinkable, has suffered and has been harmed but who is still watching over the people who ride this train. *La Volcana* protects the undocumented unaccompanied minors.

There is a sun and a moon evidencing the many days and nights that the migrants traveled through. Most of them had lost count of how many days had passed between leaving their countries and being detained and taken to the prison. The image of the sculpture known as *El Salvador del Mundo*/The World Savior which is erected in the heart of San Salvador, El Salvador, appears in the mural towards the left of a crucifixion. The inclusion of these religious figures talks less about dogma and more about how the young men and women who participated in this project saw themselves or friends and family of theirs who had succumbed to violence. They saw themselves as victims of a system that would choose to harm them before supporting them, both in Central America and in the United States. No one seemed to care about who they were as individuals. No one trusted that they would become adult men and women, caring, responsible, and able to be contributors of a history in which they could partake actively.

Emiliano Zapata and Chief Lempira, leaders of resistance in Mexico and Honduras, are standing behind the rusty train as if protecting it in this unfathomable journey. Zapata led the Mexican Revolution and Lempira, "Lord of the Mountains" with an army of 30,000 men, fought against the Spanish occupation. None of them were, ultimately, victorious. But both of them, tried to defend that which was unquestionably theirs. In their struggle they had lost land, power, and lives, but they never relinquished their pride and their dignity. Pride, dignity, and hope is the fuel that feeds *La Bestia* carrying men and women who are determined to have a better future than the atrocious past they had left behind. The oxidized-orange train has seven windows each of which tells a story.

As if entering a stage from right to left, the mural captures personal histories narrated visually in each of the windows.

Window #1

A fifteen-year-old Honduran girl from San Pedro Sula escaped from her house when she learned that her brother had been killed by members of an adversary gang. She knew that the close kinship with her brother would make her suspect and, very likely, a victim of the unstoppable escalation of violence that she had witnessed in her community. She was frightened. She left in such a rush that she had not told her mother about her escape. It tormented her to imagine that her mother may have assumed that she was dead.

She had heard of the women killed in the desert. Mostly, they were young and poor like herself. They worked in assembly plants, *maquilado-*

ras, and disappeared after leaving work. After having been missing for days, weeks, or months their skeletal remains were usually discovered in the yellow vastness of the desert. These were the dead and disappeared women from Ciudad Juárez.

The train she boarded in Ixtepec left her close to Ciudad Juárez. For some time, she followed a group of men and one woman going north. She distrusted the men and was suspicious of the woman who did not show any sign of welcoming. For two days, she walked alone. She passed out several times, thirsty and hungry beyond words. She run into a man who seemed kind enough for her to believe that he would take her to safety. It could have been that she was desperate, or perhaps the man was well accustomed to lying. She followed him. The kind man was part of a drug cartel dominating the border in the north of the state of Chihuahua. The Honduran girl hardly knew that she was becoming victim of human trafficking. She suffered sexual abuse. She was "sold" in Mexico and forced into prostitution.

Now in prison in the United States, the Honduran young woman wondered if death back home would have not been a better choice than the long and painful rosary of tragic events that shaped her journey north.

Window #2

A sixteen-year old Mexican boy from Michoacán was visiting his cousin from his mother's side. He knew that this older cousin had been involved in some shady business of which neither he nor his family ever talked about. The cousin had a missing finger. No one dared to ask how he had lost it. They were in a festive mood when they decided to go to a near-by bar for beers and some music. Because it was still early, the bar was almost empty, people spoke in calm and friendly voices.

The Michoacán boy could not remember where exactly the

armed men came from. It could have not been from the main entrance of the building because he was facing that direction and saw no one blowing up the door. The shooting was so loud and so fast that the only thing he tried, and was unable to do, was to hide under a table. Before he was able to locate his cousin, he was taken by two men into a car, his head was covered with a hood that impeded him seeing where he was taken to. The cousin and the Michoacán boy were pushed out of the cars, beaten badly with metal rods. The cousin, now on his knees, was asking for forgiveness. He had nothing to do with the death of one of the cartel members. The Michoacán boy was petrified by fear. He could hardly feel the burning pain of a sharp knife cutting his upper torso.

There was a solid sound that he had never heard before. It was not loud. It was demolishing in its precise intent. His cousin was shot in the abdomen while on his knees. The Michoacán boy had never seen the exploded insides of a person. For incomprehensible associations, he thought that it looked like a bloody soup.

The body of his cousin he never saw again. The men took the Michoacán boy to a dilapidated, disgustingly smelly latrine. The floor was earth. He dug his way out during the night. No one saw him running and crying. Somehow, he got to Tijuana. He was in hiding for few weeks until he decided to cross the United States–Mexico border.

Window #3

A fourteen-year-old Salvadoran boy divided the square shape that defined the window he worked on into symmetrical parts. He spent concentrated time making sure that the two parts would be exactly equal. The right side of his image was mostly depicted in grays. There are weapons, a jail, a threatening sky frames the image. The left side, by contrast, is light and sunny, a rainbow crosses the image from right to left. Although the Salvadoran artist had grown up in San Salvador, a congested, loud and densely populated city, he still remembered his mother talking about Chalatenango where she was from and where she wanted to return someday.

She never managed to make that trip to her hometown. She died when the Salvadoran boy was ten years old. He had an older brother who was involved in the *Mara Salvatrucha*, one of the most feared gangs in El Salvador. Her sister, who was few years older than himself, without saying a word to anyone, disappeared from the house. The Salvadoran boy thinks that she may have tried to cross to Guatemala and from there to Mexico and to the United States. He got involved in a gang that was not the one his brother belonged to. Mostly, he had joined that other one because he was so hungry that when they offered him some *tortillas con frijoles*, he did not think it twice.

His involvement with crime was so precipitous and unchosen, that he recognized in the painting of his window on the train, that although he is definitely part of the gray landscape, he deserves to have a second chance and a better, brighter future. After all, he said, he was only fourteen.

Window #4

A sixteen-year-old boy from Honduras, proud of his African-Honduran roots and his *Garífona* ancestry painted on the mural the only reality that he could think of, what he was facing now. This jail, this confinement, this enclosure that was eroding his soul. He shared that he was constantly cold for the uninterrupted air-conditioning in 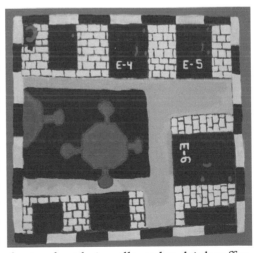 the prison. He was hungry and missed not being allowed to drink coffee. He tried, and most of the times managed, to be well behaved because he detested and resented being taken to solitary confinement. He did not want to remember where he was coming from. He could not imagine where he was going to. His days and nights were a long, boring, punishing sequence of nothingness.

He got along with most of his eight members "pod" cohort but trusted no one. He tried to remain aloof, painfully detached whenever he was insulted or provoked. It was not worthy acting out at the exchange of risking being taken to solitary confinement. He deserved better.

Window #5

A beautiful portrait of a Madonna emerged. The artist was a sixteen-year-old Guatemalan boy, with friendly eyes and a voice so soft that was almost inaudibly. He painted the image of the Virgin Mary not because of its religious symbol for he had never been Catholic or a believer. He wanted to allude to the suffering of women who are being murdered senselessly, daily, in Guatemala. He honored mothers who witnessed their own children being killed.

He was only nine years old when he was abandoned by his mother and father. He did not know why they left him alone in the market and never returned to look for him. He suspects or wants to believe, or both, that it was because they could not feed the five younger siblings he had. He had no family and lived by himself on the streets of Guatemala City. He could not retrieve the name of the small community where he had lived somewhere in Quiché. The only intact memory he still had from his childhood, which he treasured, was that of his older sister Ixcanil who took care of him for a while. She had killed herself two years before he was abandoned in the market.

Window #6

It was hard to leave Honduras. It was hell to cross the border. Now he was in prison in the United States. Why so much had gone wrong? What he wanted the most now was to return to Siguatepeque. It is not a nice city, it is overcrowded, noisy, and filthy, but everyone spoke Spanish and would understand that he was from there. He was sixteen years old when he entered the prison. He hoped he would be released before becoming eighteen. If he managed to return, he would make a pact with himself and others to live in calm. In peace.

His dream had always been to have a store that would sell all kind of goods. He would not sell stolen goods. He had realized already that crime only leads to more crime. He would inaugurate a movie house where he would be involved in choosing the films that would be shown to kids and young people like himself. *Rambo* and violent movies would be fine because the violence depicted in those films was different and more benevolent than the real shooting and kidnapping, the dismembering and burying people alive that he had seen in his trip on *La Bestia*.

He would build a discotheque that would be open 24 hours a day. Managing businesses was something that, of course, he had never done. But he felt confident that he could learn and prosper.

Window #7

He grew up among people who told him that he had a good voice. He was invited to sing in parties and friend's weddings and, although he had never learned to play an instrument, there was always someone available to accompany him with a guitar, making people clap and laugh.

He was sixteen years old, from Honduras. Originally from a small rural community but he had lived most of his life in Tegucigalpa. It was there where he got involved in gangs, not knowing, really, what he was doing.

When he finally learned, it was almost too late. He had run away. It was nothing short from a miracle that he had not been killed already. He had not plan to cross the United States–Mexico border. He kept on escaping north to be far from the Honduran gang that was chasing him. He still wanted to become a singer. He imagined his voice reaching far villages in Honduras. The lyrics of his songs would be inspired in what happened to him and to his friends. Yes, they would be sad songs of longing and violence, but they would be true. He hoped that people would listen.

The train enters a tunnel that, unlike most, is not dark and unknown. This passageway is flooded with light, it seems transparent. There is text that decorates the walls of this welcoming aperture. The word FAITH written in many languages brings beauty, hope and a possible alternative to a better future. Young men and women are seated on The Beast's roof. This is an unsafe, brutal journey. People will be robbed or killed before reaching the border. Women will be raped. They will be submissive because sexual violence would be perceived as a better option than being pushed out of the train, having arms or legs amputated. Few will arrive safely to the United States.

This project was completed in less than three weeks. The mural was beautiful and celebrated. The participating artists were visibly proud when they introduced the concluded mural to the deputy director, councilors, and guards. They were eager to know when they could start a new mural after having enjoyed working on this one. I returned to my home, to the routine of preparing dinner, visiting friends, or planning an upcoming trip. But I could not abandon the thought of the youth in prison, submissive under the imposed unbending reality that was designing their life within the United States criminal justice system. How long would it take until they would be free? This was an abrasive consideration that felt as if I was holding an incandescent stone that burned and injured me. The distance between the undocumented unaccompanied Central American incarcerated minors and everyone else outside that confinement seemed to me astronomically apart.

I had learned about these young men and women through the fragile circumstances that brought us together to create an extraordinary art piece. Had it not been because of the mural project, I would have never learned about their lives and what they had already seen, experienced, touched or about the violent reality of depravation that they had been exposed to.

In 2018, over 66,000 unaccompanied, undocumented, migrant Central American children and youth crossed the United States–Mexico border. In 2019, an estimated 600 undocumented unsupervised children and youth crossed the border daily.

This mural was oral history made visual tracing whispers of unspoken words and following steps on the vastness of yellowed desert sands from Central America to Mexico and to the United States. Borders, real or imposed, geographic, cultural, or religious frontiers that fracture the social texture of communities all over the world, need urgent reconsideration to accommodate a reality of *limits* that must become permeable, inclusive, welcoming.

La Bestia/The Beast. Mural on canvas. Photograph by Claudia Bernardi.

The Language of Water

Lee Peterson

> *"Then I began to say what I believe."*
> M. Rukeyser's The Life of Poetry

We talk about migrants but not
the bones of feet—*talus*, which is also
a mass of rock at the foot of a cliff;
cuneiform, which is also an ancient Mesopotamian,
Persian, and Ugaritic form of writing; *navicular*,
which also means "boat-shaped."

We should talk less of boats, of lack
and need. (Though these are all the same.)
We should talk about how lungs under X-rays
look like leaves under sunlight, how the veins
of each spread out like the veins of river beds.
About the pulse in a finger pad or nail bed.

We talk of tearing hands from other hands,
about invasions of bodies over land.
But we should speak more about the way
sweat thickens between palms,
the way a womb thickens, preparing
to host life, preparing to shed it.

We cannot talk about refugees and not
talk about war or water. About the breath
into and out of the mouth and how this is union.
The precise pulmonological term
for visual evidence of disease is "sign."
There are many types, many signs:

Haystack sign. Hilium convergence sign.
Holly leaf sign. Finger in glove. Flat waist.
Ginko leaf. Golden S. Incomplete border.
Juxtaphrenic peak. Melting ice cube. More black.
Sillouette. Steeple. Spinaker. Straight left heart border.
Third mogul. Walking man. Water bottle. Wave.

We must name what we don't know
before we pretend at what we do.
When we talk about migrants
we should breathe more and talk less.
But if we must talk, we should speak
in the language of water.

Chalk / *La Tiza* (A One-act Play)

Catalina Florina Florescu

IUSE THIS PIECE TO protest against virulent cruelty in which some people are treated like they do not have any rights and are consequently scarred emotionally for life. On the other hand, I admire institutions, agencies, and people who have embraced Deferred Action for Childhood Arrivals (DACA) and immigrants knowing that a place is as much fluid and alive as it allows people from various backgrounds to co-exist.

Dedicated to those who died in my country in 1989 so I could live free in exile.

Dedicated to my DACA students at Pace University and to my son whose parents came to the United States first to study, then to stay.

Characters

ALEGRÍAS: 35 years old.
SOCIAL WORKER WOMAN 1: 20 years old.
SOCIAL WORKER WOMAN 2: early 30s.
I.C.E. OFFICERS *qua* shadow puppets.
ALEGRÍAS' PARENTS in V.O.

Setting

A classroom at a university in the United States.

Time

Sometime a little bit in the future plus flashbacks.

Act One

An actor enters. He is well dressed. The setting resembles a college classroom. The entire audience members are seated on chairs similar to those in college classrooms. There is a board, ideally circular in shape (enveloping the classroom *qua* stage). Above the board, equally enveloping, there is a reflective surface (a mirror), so all participants are seen. There are many pieces of chalk. All are white. The man goes to the board and starts drawing a map, clouds, birds, people, barbwire, and writes LA FRONTERA. Projected, we see footage from the news with people walking to get to the United States–Mexico border. Then, silence. He returns to the board and erases several letters. Now LA FRONTERA has become TIERRA.

ALEGRÍAS: Good afternoon. I have told this story many times to my students, my kids, strangers whom I meet in the street. I will tell it until I die. My name is Alegrías. Well, it's not my birth name; it's a nickname. You see my parents were deported when I was a boy. During their short life in the States they were farm cropping, toilet cleaning, dish washing, poorly paid, and poorly treated people. I remember … [hesitatingly], I think this happened to me. Sometimes it's hard to confirm my own past, especially since I was raised without parents. Look, this *tiza* saved *mi vida*. [*Kisses it.*] My parents used to call me Alegrías and when I asked them why, they said:

V.O. FATHER: Well, son, that's easy. You made us happy.

ALEGRÍAS: I asked them, "Why is this the only Spanish word you say to me?" My mother did not say a word and I heard father whispering something in Spanish to her, but back then I did not speak my parents' mother tongue. I remember asking them, "Why don't you teach me your birth language?" My question always remained unanswered. Almost every time I asked it, I heard dad saying to mom:

V.O. FATHER: Mujer, cállate!

ALEGRÍAS: They were afraid to speak their native language. Afraid to hear:

V.O. MOTHER: Go back to your country, beaners!

V.O. FATHER: Listen, son, learn English, so no one will ever question your place of birth.

ALEGRÍAS: But, father, in school they teach us to pay respect to our ancestors.

V.O. FATHER [*Skeptical.*] Sure, they say that devouring our food. But reality has more than one face.

ALEGRÍAS: What do you mean?

V.O. FATHER: Just learn, get good grades, and never look back. The past is the heaviest burden of all.

ALEGRÍAS: Father, are you OK?

V.O. FATHER: Yeah, yeah, I am fine. Go to bed now.

[ALEGRÍAS *goes back to the board and points emphatically to the word* TIERRA.]

ALEGRÍAS: My parents could never look straight into my eyes and admit their mistake, or guilt, or just be brutally honest and tell me why they did not teach me Spanish. So, I had to change my strategy. I asked them once about my extended family. My father was a gentle man passing for a tough one; his hands were cracked because of manual labor in dusty fields; his soles were growing another layer of skin from all those miles that he walked from work to home. I remember him saying I did not have anyone else but them. He always looked into my eyes and said that if anyone asked about my family I should say without pausing:

V.O. FATHER: [*In a very rapid way.*] We are all fine, thank you, who wants ice cream?

ALEGRÍAS: You know why, right? Because this is a culture where things are hidden. It appears welcoming and emancipated, but that is just one superficial level. Besides, asking kids about ice cream would have been a detour from their staring at me. [*Beat.*] Growing up, I learned I had to be someone else. My mother once pulled me aside and said:

V.O. MOTHER: Son, this is for you. Take this mask.

ALEGRÍAS: What? Why?

V.O. MOTHER: Back in my village, women were doing chores together, laughing and crying as one. When I came to America I could not sleep for months. It was so silent, it felt like a graveyard. Every night I put myself to sleep reminiscing all the women's laughs I heard back home. They were like lullabies. One day, a coworker was looking for her pack of cigarettes and a mask slipped off of her bag. I asked what that was for. She said it was for her daughter who was a fox in a school's end-of-the-year show. The woman said I should try it. I asked why and she said it's good when you can't find your words; or when you want to be someone else. She said her daughter taught her that trick. For a moment I stood with that mask in front of my face and nothing came out of my mouth. I told her jokingly the mask must be broken. She said, "No, querida, you are." Maybe it was the word querida that women back home used to call one another, maybe it was something else, but all of a sudden I could not stop these words coming out of me: Mira, soy una mujer cansada. Esta tierra no está llena de sueños. No son mis sueños de todos modos. Pero hay demasiada pobreza y inseguridad en mi propio país. No hay punto de retorno. Nunca oiré a esas mujeres llorar y reír. Nunca.

ALEGRÍAS: Mom, that was so beautiful. What does it mean?

V.O. MOTHER: It's too complicated.

ALEGRÍAS: Please, tell me.

V.O. MOTHER: Tierra, that means land. I'll teach you more tomorrow.

ALEGRÍAS: Tierra, tierra, tierra. [*Beat.*] I was intoxicated by the sound of that word. I was spinning, holding tierra in my heart. You see I grew up being loved by my parents. But they were very tired and consumed by sadness. They were homesick. They were afraid for me. They warned me that I should never reveal my nickname and once I almost betrayed them. I was at school, playing during recess and I said: "Las alegrías, las alegrías … ." A kid asked me, "What did you just say?" I panicked, I replied in a hurry, my voice splitting in distress, as if followed by shadowy monsters: "Nothing, nothing. I must have heard this in a dream." He was piercing me with his eyes. He almost called another kid, but I said immediately, "Do you want ice cream?"

[*He returns to the board and writes* SUEÑO.]

ALEGRÍAS: We are all caught in one sueño. A dream that is yet so different from person to person. Mine ended abruptly.

[*He goes off stage. He comes back wearing pajamas. He holds a blanket in his hands.*]

ALEGRÍAS: One night, there was a knock on the door. It became louder and louder.

[*We hear a loud knock.*]

ALEGRÍAS: I saw men wearing uniforms on which I could read the letters I, C, and E, like in "ice," but no cream. They were holding their hands on rifles, yelling:

I.C.E. OFFICER 1: Open up!

I.C.E. OFFICER 2: Are you Fernando Borrador?

V.O. FATHER: Yes, sir, I am.

ALEGRÍAS: They pushed my father out of bed. They did not bother to ask my mother's name. They pushed her out of bed, too. They did not see me.

I.C.E. OFFICER 2: [*Disrespectful.*] A wetback always marries a wetback.

ALEGRÍAS: He laughed maniacally and then spat on the laadi, the very old rug my mother brought from Mexico, her dowry when she got married and crossed the border. I poked my head out of the blanket and screamed, "Mom! Dad!" An officer approached me. My mom was trembling, almost fainting.

V.O. MOTHER: Do not take the child, please! I beg of you.

ALEGRÍAS: They pushed and ordered her to:

I.C.E. OFFICERS: Shut the fuck up!

[*Man makes a step forward.*]

ALEGRÍAS: Do you know how many times mi madre was told to shut up? Imagine the stories she could have been able to share, now all gone. A deleted history. Mine. And hers. And ours. Like these ephemeral drawings [*points to the board*], you see them now, but after my class there is another and another. If I forget to erase them, the school janitor does not.

[*Man returns to his previous spot.*]

ALEGRÍAS: That night the men started to whisper something. I was not scared because nothing made sense and when nothing makes sense, call it survival skill, I do not worry. I think I said to myself that I must be dreaming a mal sueño. It will go away. [*Beat.*] This sueño is horrible though and would not go away. I heard my mother:

V.O. MOTHER: Please, leave the child here, I beg of you. He is a DACA protected under the law.

ALEGRÍAS: The men laughed so hard, the walls of our place were shaking.

I.C.E. OFFICER 2: Protected??? Huh, woman, you ... [*talks to his colleague*] yo, Mike, you used to date that hot Mexican chick ... How do you say very crazy to a bitch?

I.C.E. OFFICER 1: Perra, that's bitch. Muy loca, perra.

I.C.E. OFFICER 2: [*To the woman.*]: Listen, *loca*, this is a new administration, so law, shmlaw ... Yo, Mike, was your crazy bitch from Mexico as dumb as this one? [*Laughs.*]

V.O. MOTHER: But my son is a dreamer.

I.C.E. OFFICER 1: [*Stern.*] Ma'am, be quiet! We are the law, not you.

I.C.E. OFFICER 3: [*Panting as he enters.*] What's the holdup? I told you to be done as fast as I pee. I'm done. You?

I.C.E. OFFICER 2: Yep, done. [*Yelling.*] Out, now!

I.C.E. OFFICER 3: We have to catch a hundred by dawn. That's the order we got.

ALEGRÍAS: [*Aside.*] Catch them? Were they talking about invisible fish in an invisible pond?

V.O. FATHER: [*Stage whispering*] Son, your mother and I will be crossing. Do not be afraid. We will be crossing a piece of land.

ALEGRÍAS: My mother nodded holding back tears. She knew that she had to make herself shut up for my sake. The tears were all going inside her body in chunks, I could see them traveling with difficulty inside her body. I did not cry. The last thing my parents, now in chains, said to me was:

V.O. MOTHER: Mi querido, mamá te ama.

V.O. FATHER: Papá también.

ALEGRÍAS: My parents were pushed out of our place and I heard them saying, while the van was revving up its engine:

V.O. MOTHER AND FATHER: Alegrías, Alegrías, take care of you, hijo ...

ALEGRÍAS: The words were disappearing taking my parents and childhood away with them. I stayed in bed for days. I had water and something to eat. One day, there was a knock on the door. I rushed to answer thinking my parents were brought back to me: "Mom! Dad! You are home!" I opened the door. Two women were standing there holding a file.

SOCIAL WORKER WOMAN 1: Hi, are you William Frank Moses Borrador?

ALEGRÍAS: Yes.

SOCIAL WORKER WOMAN 1: [*To the other woman ignoring the boy.*] This kid ... his parents really tried hard with all the names.

SOCIAL WORKER WOMAN 2: Tried what hard?

SOCIAL WORKER WOMAN 1: Sometimes I wonder if you are dumb on purpose.

ALEGRÍAS: [*Aside*] Hearing that word, I can't explain why, made me smile.

SOCIAL WORKER WOMAN 1: [*Superior.*] Look, William sounds American, Frank German, and Moses, well, this one has a touch from the Holy Bible. But then, boom, Borrador, the identity is revealed in an instant. Betrayed by the family name. You can't run away from who you were born to be.

ALEGRÍAS: [*Aside*] I edited that in my head and was left with, "Betrayed by my family name ... [*slowly*] ... my family name ... [*extremely slow*] ... betrayed." [*Loud to them.*] Hello?

SOCIAL WORKER WOMAN 1: [*Shaking her head.*] Yes, yes, we see you. [*Looking in the file.*] Not good ... Not good at all.

SOCIAL WORKER WOMAN 2: Didn't you study the case at home? Who's dumb now?

SOCIAL WORKER WOMAN 1: Your parents are gone, right?

ALEGRÍAS: Yes. When are they coming back?

SOCIAL WORKER WOMAN 1: They are not.

SOCIAL WORKER WOMAN 2: Not right now, little one. Take this lollipop.

ALEGRÍAS: Thanks. Where are my parents?

SOCIAL WORKER WOMAN 1: [*Indifferent.*] Who knows?

SOCIAL WORKER WOMAN 2: We do not know. We are looking for them.

SOCIAL WORKER WOMAN 1: [*Sarcastic.*] Yeah, we are. That's our government's top priority.

ALEGRÍAS: What?

SOCIAL WORKER WOMAN 2: You are safe.

ALEGRÍAS: But I am scared and I am hungry.

SOCIAL WORKER WOMAN 2: You are not alone, you know?

ALEGRÍAS: Yes, I am.

SOCIAL WORKER WOMAN 2: Here, in this house you are. But we came to take you …

ALEGRÍAS: [*Hopeful*] … to my parents?

SOCIAL WORKER WOMAN 1: Kid, your parents are gone.

SOCIAL WORKER WOMAN 2: Until we find them, we are going to take you to a place where there are many kids and toys.

ALEGRÍAS: I do not want toys. I want my parents.

SOCIAL WORKER WOMAN 1: Hurry up. Pack a few things and let's go. We need to make nine more stops.

SOCIAL WORKER WOMAN 2: Yes, that is true. We need to save other kids.

ALEGRÍAS: Are you angels?

SOCIAL WORKER WOMAN 2: Something like that.

SOCIAL WORKER WOMAN 1: Our government made a huge mess but we clean after it.

SOCIAL WORKER WOMAN 2: Kid, let me help you pack. Anything special you want to take with you?

ALEGRÍAS: This … [*points to the rug*]. My parents are not bad people. Where are they?

SOCIAL WORKER WOMAN 1: We really don't know, kid. I am sorry.

As he packs his things, we are going to see a video with a family, a mother, a father, a child in the kitchen making alegrías. They sing in Spanish and are happy. When the video stops, the man is covered in that blanket.

ALEGRÍAS: I used to cook alegrías with my parents. I used to stick my fingers in the dough. It had toasted amaranth seeds and honey and, for a second, we stayed together like that. I will never forget that moment. We touched our hands amid that stickiness. It was beautiful. Now I am wrapping my body and mind, inside and outside, with that memory. Nobody can take that away from me. It's forever mine, like my eyes that are my mother's and my hair that is my father's.

[*Man goes off stage and comes back wearing a sarape.*]

ALEGRÍAS: My name is William Frank Moses Borrador. You can call me Alegrías, too, but only after you have said my full name. I am 35 years old. After my parents were taken away, I grew up in a foster care system. I lived with many families. I was docile, following orders, but somehow I was relocated constantly. I learned Spanish in secret. I had this plan to learn, get a job, find my parents, travel to Mexico, and bring them back here. Time passed and I became a naturalized American. Everything was planned to perfection. I knew when I would meet them I would say: Mamá, papá, qué alegría haberlos finalmente encontrado. Nadie nos va a separar de nuevo. That was the plan: to find them and talk to them in their mother tongue. To end the night that separated us reunited by words in Spanish. [*Looking at audience.*] Beautiful dream, right? But two weeks before I was supposed to board the plane, I got a call.

[*This next part is recorded. The man seems to be out of his body, something that he must have experienced way too many times. He pushes press on his phone.*]

RECORDING: Hola, soy el alcalde de Teotitlán del Valle. ¿Puedo hablar con el señor Borrador? Hablando. Lo siento, pero tus padres murieron. ¿Que? Lo siento mucho, pero están muertos.

ALEGRÍAS: My parents died in a car accident. A truck drove over them. Have you ever travelled to bury your parents? Instead of embraces and kisses, your hands are empty, your soul is devastated. How many times does a person have to lose their parents? How many times will I wake up in the middle of the night shivering with fear, reliving the night when I saw my parents for the last time? And who is responsible for this nightmare?

[*He goes to the board and writes again* LA FRONTERA. *Returns and faces the audience.*]

ALEGRÍAS: [*Holding a piece of chalk.*] This piece saved me. When my parents were snatched in the middle of the night, all I remember was how they used to call me in the house, Alegrías. I found a piece of chalk under bed. I started to draw to survive. I had to do something to make sure I will not lose my mind. I needed to feel I was not abandoned. This piece made me travel. I was not alone because of it.

[*He goes to the board and writes* BORRADOR. *Returns center stage.*]

BORRADOR: Hola, my name is Borrador. It means eraser in Spanish. You can't erase me. You can't erase my past. My history class is about to start. Would you like to stay?

[*He hands a piece of chalk to someone from the audience.*]

BORRADOR: [*Instructing that volunteer.*] Write the word you are most scared of and then give the chalk to someone else. [*To the audience.*] Un pedazo de tiza me salvo la vida. Let us speak. Ahora.

[*We hear a school bell ringing three times.*]

END OF PLAY

When the East and the West Collapse: Poetry and Ruminations on Immigration, Exile, and Refuge

Roxana Cazan

I WAS BORN IN ROMANIA at a time when the nation was beginning to shake off the last feathers of Communist complacency, like a molting bird.[1] My parents were poor. We lived in a small apartment in downtown Sibiu, close to the grocery store. White shelves trembled empty under the weight of dust, and bored store attendants gossiped about food rations, abortions, and the countryside. Put in charge of keeping an eye out for the delivery truck, the children of the neighborhood would announce its arrival with shrill calls, "Food is here!" Then, the adults would rush to the store and wait in a line hoping there'd be enough chicken feet or bologna for everyone. My homemade clothes spun vivid colors and reflected an intimate *haute couture* because my aunt was a knitting genius and my grandfather a skilled furrier. For having sold his fur coats to Western clients, my intrepid grandfather spent six months in a Danube Delta prison where his cell was always flooded up to his ankles. I was nine when the anti-Communist revolutionaries (who were the terrorists?) took to the streets in the evening of December 21, 1989, only a month after the fall of the Berlin Wall, and demanded democracy by dusk. My father fought, felt a gun against his head, and took my family into hiding. My mother grabbed all the meat in the house and cooked a pot of *sarmale* for the folks in the street. Righteous "terrorists,"[2] my parents wanted me to remember this life and be grateful for what we had even if we didn't have enough.

---

1 In 1989, the Romanian Revolution ended the Communist rule in Romania.

2 The term "terrorists" was first used by Nicolae Ceauşescu to refer to the Romanian citizens who marched in Timişoara in 1989. The term was also used by the Communist government to refer to those who opposed the party and the country's leader. They were depicted as criminals, ready to kill innocent citizens. In truth, anyone could have been deemed a "terrorist" if suspected to be of anti-Communist leaning. Because my father was caught running in the street, the Securitate (the secret police) thought he was hiding something. They caught him and forced him to admit he was a terrorist. Fortunately, the person interrogating him believed him when he explained he was running to get his children home and let him go.

For the past sixteen years, I have been living in the United States. I moved homes over twenty times. I lived in four states, pursuing my graduate education and my career. I obtained four graduate degrees. I purchased and sold two homes. I filed my taxes every year. I gathered family around me. I have felt both "Eastern" and "Western," two concepts I am not entirely sure I understand or like. And yet, living as an immigrant has been the hardest thing I have ever done. I tried to define this difficulty in the poem below.

bleat

n.

1. The characteristic utterance of goats or sheep; a sound similar to their cry.
   a. My grandfather raised two gray goats. The goats had earrings shaped like knives to plot ancestry.
   b. I was born during that terrible draught, a meat-monger, a mouse atoning for its hunger.
2. Like me, every animal had to prove their usefulness. Unbutton their bodies for the country, like women their wombs.
   a. My mother was like a chicken full of eggs. Every year, she'd cannonball one.
   b. Catch it before it hatched, the cleaver plunking to cut all vessels before sunrise.
   c. Two survived. I became a sea song. My body became a shark with silver teeth harpooned into the shore,
   d. but the country did not want a rotten girl.

v. **bleated, bleating, bleats**

v.intr.

1. To cry yourself to sleep on a boat or a plane. Border benches are not all painted yellow.
   a. I wanted everyone to drown inside me. I was so lonely, I wanted to pickle my tongue.
   b. According to my mother, it was best to find a man soon, have my breasts bitten into like plums.
   c. On the other side of the ocean, I revisited its shoreline. The sea was almost dry.
   d. I found dregs of people, dry like shed skin. They came afloat like men-of-war.
2. To whine, when you cannot hold the grief in. I can only hold my breath for a little while. I cannot swim well.

    a. At some point I forgot the language. Words become dumb
       butterflies.
    b. At some point, I rerouted my veins. They had to reach a safe place.
    c. At some point.

Although I have never been "othered" on account of my accent or my country of origin, postcolonial scholars have investigated how modernity determined the definitions of "Eastern" and "Oriental" in relation to the West.[3] In the context of Eastern Europe, Cold War politics and the attendant presumptions of Orientalist contamination, Balkanization, and a general barbarism serve to distance the East from the West. This subtext underwrites the representations of modern Romanian identities in the United States that often conjure images of orphan children, stray dogs, or undocumented immigrants.[4] This representational repertoire of Eastern Europeans was particularly prominent during the Cold War period, and so little did I expect to see it reemerge albeit abruptly in 2017.

A newspaper article published online in early July 2017 by a large Pittsburgh daily described the anger aroused in the small community of California, PA by a group of about 40 undocumented Romanian immigrants who disrupted the expected demographic tableau in the region. (The article was taken down the next day, and its replacement clarified that these people were not only Romanian but also Romani/Gypsy). A few noticeable right-wing media outlets began to describe the controversy in the following days, referring to the residents' complaints to reporters that these Romanian newcomers are disruptive and uncivilized, trashing their own yards, beheading chickens, and defecating in public. Fox News, Breitbart, The Blaze, Gateway Pundit, Tucker Carlson, and Alex Jones picked up this news incident and began pushing stories about Gypsies from Romania unwilling and unfit for US settlement.

Much of the vituperative and ignorant language sanctioned by some media pundits helped unearth a highly problematic public discourse,

---

3   From Edward Said to Maria Todorova, scholars have noted that being Eastern has consistently meant standing in opposition to the West.

4   Valentina Glajar and Domnica Radulescu have pointed out how women from Eastern Europe appear in the Western imagination as "wretches, as manly or Amazon-like, as naïve and innocent, and as alluring slightly Oriental or exotic temptresses with an edge of vampirism … , [or as] miserable babushkas" (6–7). Such attitudes contribute to understanding Romanians as "not quite European," and loosely associated with a stereotypically ambiguous and retrograde Orient.

which became visible in online comments posted by readers. Several of these contributors used the ethnic appellatives "Romanian" and "Armenian" interchangeably (see the comments to the petition entitled "End Housing of Illegal Immigrants in California"). On his radio show, Alex Jones referred to Roma people as "Muslims [who will] rape your wife too" (Karet). Many of these texts employed immigration terms synonymously, calling the Romanians both "refugees" and "undocumented immigrants" alike. For instance, a Fox News online article published on July 14, 2017 called the Romanians "immigrants," while Scott Beveridge writing for the *Observer-Reporter* called them "asylum seekers" and an article on the Narrative Collapse website referred to the same community as "illegal aliens." One online post argued that the real danger these refugees bring to California, PA stems from the fact that Romania constitutes a hotbed for ISIS fundamentalist recruits. Another comment identified the headscarf worn by traditional Cortorari women as a "Muslim scarf."

Romanians began to settle in North America in the second half of the nineteenth century. Because the Austro-Hungarian Empire continued to rule Romania until World War I, many Romanian immigrants to the United States entered the country with Austro-Hungarian passports and were therefore not recognized by the US government as Romanians. Until the beginning of World War I, there is a record of 134,253 immigrants from Transylvania, 90 percent of whom were Romanian (Leuca 22). The first Romanian Jews came to America midway through the nineteenth century, between the 1860s and 1870s (Wertsman 49; Diner 81). Other waves of Romanian-Jewish immigration followed during the interwar and the Communist periods. In his *Encyclopedia of North American Immigration*, John Powell explains that emigration throughout the years of Communist rule was generally difficult, and the number of people who managed to flee the country was relatively low (257). After 1989, the borders opened up for those seeking (mainly economic) mobility (Powell 257). Over the span of a few years following the fall of Communism, the number of immigrants has increased considerably. The 91,106 registered Romanian immigrants in the United States in 1990 rose to 367,278 in 2000. In 2009, the Census Bureau's Population Estimates Program counted 518,653 Romanians in the United States, while a 2012 American Community Survey showed this number to be 462,974. However, if we account for undeclared or undocumented

Romanians, the number is probably significantly higher. The Romanian Embassy in Washington DC estimates about a million Romanians living in the United States today.[5]

I myself am a naturalized Romanian immigrant. Living in the West, however, my life has been uncomplicated. While I feel extremely grateful and proud of my new home, I know that in the United States, my race is invisible. I am privileged as a white, educated, heterosexual, middle-class woman, and I still feel uncomfortable and unprepared to write about or teach about the harrowing processes of othering, or pushing individuals into margins, stripping them of agency, and erasing their voices based on their racial, ethnic, or gendered making. I remember my best friend's quivering voice in March 2017, as she called me in panic from Bloomington, IN, the setting of our graduate school program where she was finishing up her PhD degree. Twisting her beautiful words around hiccups and sighs, she described an incident where her husband and she were asked to return to their country and called "ISIS rag heads." My friend happens to be a Muslim woman born and raised in India. Perhaps I am stretching this interpretation, but Bloomington, IN, my former home, lies some 33 miles away from Martinsville, one of the alleged Ku Klux Klan strongholds called the "sundown town" because African-American people "were expected to clear out before dark" (NPR). In Indiana, the KKK have attacked African-Americans, Jews, immigrants, the LGBTQ, and Catholics. In fact, their last rally took place in 2012. In truth, I have heard many stories.

As I think about my friend's life in Indiana, and mine in Pennsylvania, I realize two things: I am emotionally tied to my friend's community because I love her and have come to admire and adore her culture. Simultaneously, I am tied to the immigrants in California, PA because we share a common nationality and a language that continues to pull at my heart's strings, sometimes more forcefully than English. Empathy allowed me to understand the location of my own assumptions about my culture and that of others and to force uncomfortable conversations. Martha Nussbaum, Professor of Law and Ethics at the University of

---

5 Some of these research paragraphs first appeared in my dissertation, *Contested Motherhood: The Politics of Gender, Ethnicity, and Identity in Contemporary Romanian-American Literature and Culture*, Department of English, Indiana University, Bloomington, IN, July 2014.

Chicago, argues against the unexamined opinion that our preferences do not matter (Aviv). The choices we make in terms of language, humor, the texts we read, or the films we watch reflect ideologies we adopt often times uncritically. It is important that we listen and record stories of others, that we choose carefully the way we speak, the friends we make, so that our source of consciousness, the beliefs and drives that underlie it, do not exclude people who already live in the margins of our society.

So when the residents of California, PA called my people inadequate, I felt attacked. Pam Duricic, an interviewee, argued that unlike his grandparents, who "didn't come [to the United States] to raise havoc," the Romanians are not assimilating to "our laws" (Majors, Strasburg, and Behrman). To add fuel to the proverbial fire, almost a month after the meeting of 150 residents of California, PA who gathered to voice concerns about the influx of the Romanian refugees, white nationalists marched to "Unite the Right" in Charlottesville, VA on August 12, 2017. How can refugees, immigrants, and asylum seekers feel welcome when they are perceived as threatening, dangerous, or undeserving? In the 1950s, Hannah Arendt wrote that "once they left their homeland, [refugees] remained homeless; once they have left their state, the became stateless; once they have been deprived of their rights, they became rightless, the scum of the earth." In her book titled *Human Cargo: A Journey Among Refugees*, human rights journalist Caroline Moorehead argues that "the growing perception that refugees are a threatening and destabilizing force" has weakened not only asylum policies at states' levels, but also political campaign rhetoric, border control, and even the authority and efficacy of international organizations for refugee aid such as UNHCR (49).

For a number of years now, we have been reading about the "refugee crisis" that many Western nations have been confronting. This refugee crisis, however, is not new. According to Moorehead, in the 1950s and earlier, more than 40 million people were drifters, stateless, and displaced by war (34). They existed under the looming assumption created during the international conference at Evian in 1938 that the refugees are "disturbing to the general economy" (34). During the Cold War period, the idea of the "bad refugee" and that of "economic migrant" emerged. The 1990s saw war in Iraq, Chechnya, the Balkans, Rwanda, Sierra Leone, the disintegration of Somalia and many others (Moorehead 43). In the new millennium, attitudes toward "refugees have degenerated into chaos and panic" (46). Governments have "allowed asylum seekers to become scapegoats … exploited by xenophobic politicians" (46). A refugee crisis affects everyone, regardless of whether we choose to respond to it or not. It certainly affects my family in the United States, as both I and my husband are immigrants. Because he is an Iranian Kurd, he has a different visibility in the United States, and I tried to capture that in the poem below.

The Truth about Your Arrival

In the blunt crests of the Zagros Mountains, [your grandma's
dress is a dirty halo, an exit wound, her hands stained
with the slaughtered goat's blood] the men with gouged
eyes staring but knowing that hunger is hunger when the bombs
drop right on top of your empty house, but you were
not yet born then, and soon enough you broke into the body
of a man, around the time when the blares of sirens morphed
into bleats and the martyrs ate their limbs all night,
their dry bones the only sources of light. Your new government
said forgetting is like famine, so they wanted you to remember
but only slightly, to eat all your pagan gods out of grief,
to pack your bags but still want to stay in this shithole, and then
you were a young man with a diploma and a red circle like a ring of fire
around your head when they printed your photo in the paper,
a traitor with a skinny moustache, a new arrival with loose teeth
tethered to your last name. In the winter of those new years
in America, you wanted to unbutton your mouth, to domesticate
this disaster, to bring your mother to you soon, safely, but you didn't.

But above my frustration over the rejection of the Romanian Roma migrants in California, PA, or my fear for the ways in which my husband could be misunderstood or mistreated, I worry about my Romanian-Iranian-American son who was born in Oklahoma and is today only a few months old.

Why I Worry About My Unborn Child

Because the Oklahoma sky also stretches
Stippled with wind-bruised stars.

Because a Pakistani-American doctor came in
shuffling paperwork and ultrasounds.

Because the ocean dipped
as bodies were being pulled out of water.

Because I wake to feel you squirming,
like a fish drifting in the ocean of my body.

Because I learn of you every day, son,
whom I know nothing about,

while the woman across the street loses hers
to border detention, now coated in forged half-light.

Because of these elections and the last ones,
and the ones in which I wasn't allowed to vote.

Because your mother is an immigrant
Who saw the iron curtain fall with a bang,

and your father, another immigrant, cannot fit
the word "steak" in his mouth without an accent.

Because it's still unclear whether you'll wear
their history of bones caving in,

as if the man you will likely become
can apostrophe the pain of home-county

instead of passing for someone who can
quietly swim in, practice folding this country's damp

bed sheet like someone who understands,
standing somewhere under a sky stippled with bruised stars.[6]

---

6   This poem first appeared on the *Festival of Poetry* website, December 4, 2019.

Recently, a UNHCR study determined that out of the 65.3 million people displaced from their homes and countries by war, over 15 million are Middle Eastern: 11 million Syrian, 4 million Iraqi, and thousands North African people. Some 33,952 people flee their homes every day (UNHCR). About half of these refugees today are under eighteen years of age, and of these about five percent are unaccompanied minors (Moorehead 46). Most of these people end up living in refugee camps, where the inhumane conditions transform these places into sites for the degradation of human beings. In Europe, refugees are not welcome. In 2015, 5400 Middle Eastern refugees settled down in the camp at Calais, France and were bulldozed out not even a year later ("The Calais Jungle"). In 2016, 18,844 Middle Eastern refugees were arrested in Bulgaria (Cheresheva and Mihala). The UK resettlement program designed for single refugee children has recently been stopped, and 350 children remain in limbo (Judith Vonberg, CNN). "Italy's chief of police, Franco Gabrielli, has called for the detention and deportation of migrants, who he blames for 'instability and threats' in the country" (Judith Vonberg, CNN). The examples are overwhelming.

Both compelling and overwhelming, this data urges us, humanists, and why not, poets and writers, to act. We are called on to treat displaced individuals as people and not as numeric casualties. Politically swayed portrayals of the displaced depict them in similar ways: the displaced are terrorists. The displaced are criminals. The displaced are illegal. The displaced are different than us. However, like Nigerian writer Chimamanda Ngozi Adichie,[7] I believe that one single story cannot accurately depict the complexity of a given community, say the community of Muslim Indians or Romanian Roma in the United States. Through poetry, I write my story so that I can contribute, however little, to a complex understanding of migrant life.

7   This is in reference to Adichie's TED talk, "The Danger of a Single Story."

Sources

Americans in Lake County, Indiana." *Dissertation, University of Purdue*, 1979. https://books.google.com/books/about/Development_in_Ethnic_ Heritage_Curriculu.html?id=DeXVOwAACAAJ. Accessed 29 April, 2014.

Arendt, Hannah. *The Origins of Totalitarianism*. New York: Harcourt, 1973.

Aviv, Rachel. "The Philosopher of Feelings: Martha Nussbaum's Far-reaching Ideas Illuminate the Often Ignored Elements of Human Life—Aging, Inequality, and Emotion." *The New Yorker*, July 18, 2016, www.newyorker.com/magazine/2016/07/25/martha-nussbaums-moral-philosophies. Accessed August 14, 2019.

Beveridge, Scott. "Roma Asylum Seekers Abandon California Owing Thousands of Dollars in Back Rent," *Observer-Reporter*, Nov 3, 2017, https:// observer-reporter.com/news/localnews/roma-asylum-seekers-abandon- california-owing-thousands-of-dollars-in/article_53f44476-c0c1-11e7-aab6- 7339578b3b80.html. Accessed August 12, 2019.

Glajar, Valentina and Domnica Radulescu eds. *Vampirettes, Wretches, and Amazons: Western Representations of East European Women*, East European Monographs, 2004.

Karet, Brendan. "Conservative Media Outlets Stoke Fears That 'Gypsies' Are Coming To America and Defecating In The Streets," *Media Matters*, July 18, 2017, www.mediamatters.org/tucker-carlson/conservative-media-outlets- stoke-fears-gypsies-are-coming-america-and-defecating. Accessed August 12, 2019.

Leuca, Mary. "Development in Ethnic Heritage Curriculum; A Case Study of Romanian Americans in Lake County Indiana." *Purdue University*, 1979, PhD dissertation.

Majors, Dan, Stephanie Strasburg, and Elizabeth Behrman. "Romanians Seeking Asylum Are in California, PA as Part of U.S. Immigration Program." *Pittsburgh Post-Gazette*, July 13, 2017, www.post-gazette.com/local/ south/2017/07/14/california-pa-residents-want-answers-about-romanian- immigrants/stories/201707140150. Accessed August 12, 2019.

Moorehead, Caroline. *Human Cargo: A Journey Among Refugees*. New York: Picador, 2006.

Norris, Michelle. "Indiana Town: From Racist Past to Primary Present." NPR, April 30, 2008, www.npr.org/templates/story/story.php?storyId=90074719. Accessed August 14, 2019.

Powell, John. *Encyclopedia of North American Immigration*. New York: Facts on File, 2005.

Wertsman, Vladimir. "Romanian Jews in America: Early Immigrant Vignettes." *Multicultural Review*, 2005, pp. 49-52.

Online Sources

"Chaos after Feds Dump Dozens of Illegal Aliens on Tiny PA Town," *Narrative Collapse*, July 15, 2017, http://narrative-collapse.com/2017/07/15/chaos-after-feds-dump-dozens-of-illegal-aliens-on-tiny-pa-town/. Accessed August 12, 2019.

"End Housing of Illegal Immigrants in California." *Care2: The Petition Site*, 2017, www.thepetitionsite.com/619/689/612/end-housing-of-refugees-in-california/. Accessed August 12, 2019.

"Immigrants Defecate in Streets, Behead Chickens, Angry Pennsylvania Residents Say," *Fox News*, July 14, 2017, www.foxnews.com/us/immigrants-defecate-in-streets-behead-chickens-angry-pennsylvania-residents-say. Accessed August 12, 2019.

"Table S0201, Selected Population Profile in the United States, 2012 American Community Survey 1-Year Estimates," *United States Census Bureau*. https://factfinder.census.gov/faces/tableservices/jsf/pages/productview.xhtml?src=bkmk. Accessed May 20, 2014.

"Total ancestry reported: Total ancestry categories tallied for people with one or more ancestry categories reported 2009 American Community Survey 1-Year Estimates," *United States Census Bureau*, https://factfinder.census.gov/faces/tableservices/jsf/pages/productview.xhtml?src=bkmk. Accessed May 20, 2014.

"UNHCR Global Trends: Forced Displacement in 2017." *UNHCR*, www.unhcr.org/5b27be547.pdf. Accessed August 14, 2019.

Biographies of Contributors

Born to Jewish parents in Chile, **Marjorie Agosín** earned a BA from the University of Georgia and an MA and a PhD from Indiana University. Themes that recur in her scholarly and creative work include social justice, feminism, and remembrance. Agosín is the author of numerous works of poetry, fiction, and literary criticism, such as *The Angel of Memory* (2001), *The Alphabet in My Hands: A Writing Life* (2000), *Always from Somewhere Else: A Memoir of my Chilean Jewish Father* (1998), *An Absence of Shadows* (1998), *Melodious Women* (1997), *Starry Night: Poems* (1996), and *A Cross and a Star: Memoirs of a Jewish Girl in Chile* (1995).

Ruth Behar, the Pura Belpré Award-winning author of the coming-of-age-novel, *Lucky Broken Girl*, was born in Havana, and grew up in New York. Her books, *Translated Woman*, *The Vulnerable Observer*, *An Island Called Home*, and *Traveling Heavy* have been acclaimed as pioneering works of autoethnography. She is also the author of a bilingual book of poetry, *Everything I Kept/Todo lo que guardé*, and a historical novel, *Letters from Cuba*, based on her grandmother's escape from Poland to start a new life in Cuba. Behar was the first Latina to win a MacArthur "Genius" Grant and has been named a "Great Immigrant" by the Carnegie Corporation. She is the Victor Haim Perera Collegiate Professor of Anthropology at the University of Michigan in Ann Arbor. Additional details are at her website: www.ruthbehar.com.

Cristina A. Bejan is a Romanian-American historian, theatre artist and spoken-word poet based in Denver, Colorado. She grew up in Durham, North Carolina, and received her BA in philosophy from Northwestern University, where she also studied theatre. An Oxford DPhil and a Rhodes and Fulbright scholar, she has held fellowships at the United States Holocaust Memorial Museum, Georgetown University, and the Woodrow Wilson Center, and has taught history at Georgetown and Duke Universities, among others. She currently teaches world history at Metropolitan State University of Denver. A playwright, Bejan has written seventeen plays, many of which have been produced in the United States, Romania, the United Kingdom, and Vanuatu. She is founding executive director of the arts and culture collective Bucharest Inside the Beltway. Under the stage name "Lady Godiva," she performs her poetry across the United States and Romania. She has written *Intellectuals and Fascism in Interwar Romania: The Criterion Association* (Palgrave Macmillan, 2019) and *Green Horses on the Walls* (Finishing Line Press, 2020) and is also a contributing author for *The United States Holocaust Memorial Museum's Encyclopedia of Camps and Ghettos* Vol. 3 (University of Indiana, 2018). She has appeared on C-SPAN, and her work has been featured in the *Washington Post*, the *Huffington Post, American Prospect, Evenimentul Zilei* and *Observator Cultural*. Bejan is on the Advisory Board of Alianța and is an advocate for NAMI and RAINN. In Denver she serves as the Social Justice Director for Fearless Theatre.

Claudia Bernardi is a socially engaged and community-based artist, print-maker, and installation artist, whose artwork is influenced by the effects of war and political violence. Born in Argentina, Bernardi endured the military junta (1976–83) that caused 30,000 *desaparecidos*. Bernardi participated with the Argentine Forensic Anthropology Team in exhumations investigating human rights violations against civilians. This experience impacted her commitment to community arts. In 2005, Bernardi created the School of Art in Perquin, El Salvador, a community-based art project replicated in Sincelejo, Colombia and throughout Latin America, Switzerland, Germany, and Northern Ireland. Bernardi is professor of community arts at the California College of the Arts.

A naturalized immigrant born and raised in Romania, **Roxana L. Cazan** is the author of *The Accident of Birth* (Main Street Rag, 2017). Her poems appeared in *Connecticut River Review, Construction Magazine, Cold Creek Review, The Healing Muse, Adanna Literary Journal, Watershed Review, Allegro Poetry, The Peeking Cat Anthology, Allegro Poetry, Barnwood International Poetry Magazine, Tipton Poetry Review, The Portland Review, The Madison Review, Harpur Palate*, and others. Her translation of Matei Visniec's "Teeth" was nominated for a Pushcart Prize by *Reunion* at UT Dallas. Cazan lives in Oklahoma City, Oklahoma, where she is working on a second poetry book.

Leila Chatti is a Tunisian-American poet and author of *Deluge* (Copper Canyon Press, 2020), and the chapbooks *Ebb* (Akashic Books, 2018) and *Tunsiya/Amrikiya*, the 2017 Editors' Selection from Bull City Press. She is the recipient of scholar-ships from the Tin House Writers' Workshop, The Frost Place, and the Key West Literary Seminar, grants from the Barbara Deming Memorial Fund and the Helene Wurlitzer Foundation, and fellowships from the Fine Arts Work Center in Provincetown, the Wisconsin Institute for Creative Writing, and Cleveland State University, where she is the inaugural Anisfield-Wolf Fellow in Publishing and Writing. Her poems appear in *Ploughshares, Tin House, American Poetry Review*, and elsewhere.

Jasmin Darznik's debut novel *Song of a Captive Bird* was a *New York Times Book Review* "Editors' Choice" book and a *Los Angeles Times* bestseller. It appeared on several "best of" lists in 2018, including *Booklist, Reader's Digest*, and *Newsweek*. Darznik is also the author of the *New York Times* bestseller *The Good Daughter:*

A Memoir of My Mother's Hidden Life. Her books have been published in seventeen countries and her essays have appeared in the *New York Times, Washington Post,* and *Los Angeles Times,* among others. She has been featured in numerous academic journals, newspapers, and popular media, including National Public Radio, The Today Show, *New York Times, Newsweek, The Atlantic, Los Angeles Review, San Francisco Chronicle, Cleveland Plain-Dealer, MS., Vogue* and other national and international venues. Darznik was born in Tehran, Iran and came to the United States when she was five years old. She holds an MFA in fiction from Bennington College and a PhD in English from Princeton University. Now a professor of English and creative writing at California College of the Arts, she lives in the San Francisco Bay Area with her family. Her next book, a historical novel set in 1920s San Francisco, is forthcoming from Random House's Ballantine imprint.

Elizabeth Eslami is the author of the story collection *Hibernate,* for which she was awarded the 2013 Ohio State University Prize in Short Fiction, as well as the novel *Bone Worship* (Pegasus, 2010). Her essays, short stories, and travel writing have appeared most recently in *The Sun* and *Witness,* and her work is featured in the anthologies *Tremors: New Fiction by Iranian American Writers, The Weeklings: Revolution 1,* and *Writing Off Script: Writers on the Influence of Cinema.* She has taught in the MFA programs at Manhattanville College and Indiana University, and she is currently the Hampton and Esther Boswell distinguished professor of creative writing at DePauw University.

Catalina Florina Florescu holds a PhD in medical humanities and comparative theater conferred by Purdue University. She has authored books that are catalogued at prestigious universities (such as *Transacting Sites of the Liminal Bodily Spaces; Disjointed Perspectives of Motherhood; Transnational Narratives in Englishes of Exile; Of Silences in Munch, Beckett, Hopper, and Hanson; The Night I Burned My Origami Skin;* and *The Rebelled Body Plays*) and has been invited to give talks at Sorbonne, Columbia, New York University, Harvard, etc. She is also a playwright with volumes published bilingually and with plays currently considered for production in New York and London. She has recently switched her attention from academic to creative writing and has also joined New Jersey Theater Center where she works as a curator for New Plays Festival. More about her work can be found at her website: www.catalinaflorescu.com.

Known for mixing history with contemporary politics, **Eric J. Garcia** always tries to create art that is much more than just aesthetics. Garcia has exhibited nationally to include such institutions like the San Francisco's Museum of Modern Art, Art, the National Museum of Mexican Art and the Museum of

Contemporary Art Detroit. Received his BFA with a minor in Chicano studies from the University of New Mexico, Eric Garcia went on to completed his MFA from the School of the Art Institute of Chicago. A versatile artist working in an assortment of media, from hand-printed posters, to sculptural installations, to his controversial political cartoon series El Machete Illustrated, they all have a common goal of educating and challenging.

Eugene Garcia-Cross is the author of the story collection "Fires of Our Choosing," which was named the Gold Medal winner in the short story category by the Independent Publisher Book Awards. He's taught creative writing at Northwestern, Penn State, University of Chicago, and other institutions. His stories have appeared in *Glimmer Train, American Short Fiction, Story Quarterly,* and *Callaloo* among other publications. His work was also listed among the 2010 and 2015 Best American Short Stories' 100 Distinguished Stories. He is the recipient of scholarships from the Bread Loaf Writers' Conference, and fellowships from NBC, the National Hispanic Media Coalition, the Yaddo Artists' Colony, and the Sewanee Writers' Conference. Eugene writes for TV and lives in Los Angeles with his wife and two sons.

Kenneth Hada has seven volumes of poetry in print, including his latest: *Not Quite Pilgrims* (VAC Poetry, 2019). His work has been awarded by the National Museum of Western Heritage, Western Writers of America, SCMLA, The Writer's Almanac, and The Oklahoma Center for the Book. Additional details are at his website: www.kenhada.org.

Olga Livshin is a Russian Jewish refugee and the author of *A Life Replaced: Poems with Translations from Anna Akhmatova and Vladimir Gandelsman,* which considers immigration and translation as a trope during the Trump era. Her poetry and translations are published in the *Kenyon Review, Poetry International, Jacket* and other journals. Her recent work is recognized by *CALYX* journal's Lois Cranston Memorial Award, the Gabo Translation Prize, and other competitions, and was translated into Persian by Mohsen Emadi. She lives outside Philadelphia.

Daniel A. Lockhart is the author of four poetry collections including *Devil in the Woods* (Brick Books, 2019) and *The Gravel Lot that was Montana* (Mansfield Press, 2018). His work has appeared or is forthcoming in the *Windsor Review, Grain, Tulane Review, The Malahat Review, Contemporary Verse 2, Belt Magazine, Dalhousie Review, TriQuarterly,* and *The Journal* among others. He is a recipient of Canada Council for the Arts grant for Aboriginal People and Ontario Arts Council grants for his poetry. He work has garnered several Pushcart Prize

Nominations. He is a graduate of the Indiana University–Bloomington MFA in creative writing program where he held a Neal–Marshall graduate fellowship in creative writing. He is a member of the Moravian of the Thames First Nation.

Khaled Al-Maqtari is a Yemeni refugee living in the Markaze Yemeni Refugee Camp in Djibouti. He is married with a son. The photographs he took are meant to inform about refugees and their daily life. The subjects captured represent typical realities of life for refugees in this camp, from wind and sadness, to underprivileged childhood and dead dreams. (Nathalie Peutz, assistant professor of anthropology at New York University in Abu Dhabi, United Arab Emirates, has graciously helped us communicate with Khaled.)

The descendant of Syrian Lebanese refugees and Irish Famine migrants, **Philip Metres** has written ten books, including *Sand Opera* (2015) and *The Sound of Listening: Poetry as Refuge and Resistance* (2018), and *Shrapnel Maps* (2020). Awarded the Lannan Fellowship and two Arab American Book Awards, he is professor of English and director of the Peace, Justice, and Human Rights program at John Carroll University.

Mihaela Moscaliuc was born and raised in Romania. She is the author of the poetry collections *Immigrant Model* (University of Pittsburgh Press, 2015) and *Father Dirt* (Alice James Books, 2010), translator of Carmelia Leonte's *The Hiss of the Viper* (Carnegie Mellon University Press, 2015) and Liliana Ursu's *Clay and Star* (Etruscan Press, 2019), and editor of *Insane Devotion: On the Writing of Gerald Stern* (Trinity University Press, 2016). Her scholarship explores issues of representation, appropriation, cultural identity, exophony, and empathy. She has published essays on the works of Agha Shahid Ali, Kimiko Hahn, Shara McCallum, Colum McCann, C.K. Williams, Gerald Stern, and in the field of Romani Studies. The recipient of two Glenna Luschei Awards (in poetry and prose, respectively) from *Prairie Schooner*, residency fellowships from Chateau de Lavigny (Switzerland), Virginia Center for the Creative Arts, and the MacDowell Colony, an Individual Artist Fellowship from the New Jersey State Council on the Arts, and a Fulbright fellowship to Romania, Moscaliuc is associate professor of English at Monmouth University (New Jersey).

Matthew Murrey's poems have appeared in many journals such as *Prairie Schooner, Poetry East*, and *Rattle*. He has received an NEA Fellowship in Poetry, and his debut poetry collection, *Bulletproof*, selected by Marilyn Nelson, was published in February 2019 by Jacar Press. Murrey is a high school librarian in

Urbana, Illinois where he lives with his partner. They have two adult sons. His website is at www.matthewmurrey.net.

Bárbara Mujica is a novelist, short story writer, essayist and critic. She is the author of several novels such as *I Am Venus*, *Frida*, and *Sister Teresa*, which was adapted for the stage by Coco Blignaut, of the Actors' Studio, in Los Angeles, under the name God's Gypsy. "Gotlib, Bombero," one of Mujica's stories, was recently adapted for the stage by Ronda Spinak of the Jewish Women's Theater in Los Angeles. A professor of Spanish at Georgetown University, Mujica is a specialist in Early Modern Spanish literature and contemporary Latin American Culture. Her books on early modern literature include *A New Anthology of Early Modern Spanish Theater: Play and Playtext* (Yale University Press, 2014); editor of *Shakespeare and the Spanish Comedia* (Bucknell University Press, 2013), *Teresa de Avila, Lettered Woman* (Vanderbilt University Press, 2009), *Teresa de Jesus: Feminismo y espiritualidad* (Orto/University of Minnesota, 2007), *Women Writers of Early Modern Spain* (Yale University Press, 2004), *Et in Arcadia Ego: Essays on Death in the Pastoral Novel* (University Press of America, 1990, co-authored with Bruno Damiani), *Iberian Pastoral Characters* (Scripta Humanistica, 1986), and *Calderon's Characters: An Existential Point of View* (Puvill, 1980).

Lee Peterson's poems have appeared in such journals as *Arts & Letters*, *Salamander*, *Bellingham Review*, *The Fiddlehead*, *North American Review*, and *Meridians: Feminism, Race, Transnationalism*. A recent visitor to the faculty of Penn State University's BA/MA program in creative writing, Peterson has taught in the English and Women's, Gender, and Sexuality Studies programs at Penn State University's Altoona campus since 2004. Her collection of poems, *Rooms and Fields: Dramatic Monologues from the War in Bosnia*, was selected by Jean Valentine for the Stan and Tom Wick Poetry Prize (Kent State University Press, 2004).

Domnica Radulescu is a professor of comparative literature at a Virginia university in the USA. She holds a PhD in Romance languages from the University of Chicago. Radulescu received the 2011 Outstanding Faculty Award from the State Council of Higher Education for Virginia and is twice a Fulbright scholar. She is the author of three critically and internationally acclaimed novels: *Country of Red Azaleas* (Twelve, Hachette 2016), *Black Sea Twilight* (Doubleday 2010 & 2011) and *Train to Trieste* (Knopf 2008 & 2009) and of several plays. *Train to Trieste* has been published in thirteen languages and is the winner of the 2009 Library of Virginia Fiction Award. Two of her plays, *The Town with Very Nice People* (2013) and *Exile Is My Home: A Sci-fi Immigrant Fairy Tale* (2014) were finalists in the Jane Chambers Playwriting competition. The latter play was produced at the Theater for the New City in New York in April/May 2016 to excellent reviews. This production was also the winner of the HOLA Award for Outstanding Performance by an Ensemble Cast. Presently Radulescu is working on her fourth novel *My Father's Orchards* and has completed a memoir titled *Dream in a Suitcase: A Story of My Immigrant Life*.

Florinda Ruiz, a native of Spain, is an award-winning photographer, translator, poet, professor, and director of the Writing Program at Washington and Lee University. She holds a PhD in classics from Johns Hopkins University, has received a State Council for Higher Education in Virginia award, a US Department of Education Title VIA Grant in collaboration with Roanoke College's Modern Languages Department, and an All-College Exemplary Teaching Award at Roanoke College among other recognitions. The wide scope of her scholarship and artistic work includes topics ranging from the transmission of the Classical world in Europe, Spanish Islam, various projects on migration studies, and the convergence between visual art and poetry. Her scholarly articles have appeared in Brill's *Explorations in Renaissance Culture*, *The Sixteenth Century Journal*, and *Renaissance Studies* among others. As a translator, while she worked in the United Arab Emirates, she published the memoirs of the Sheikh of the Emirate of Sharjah and minister of Culture in the UAE, *Primeras Memorias* with Al-Qasimi Publications. Her latest publication, a chapter on "Islamic Spain After the Thirteenth Century" in *Arabic Heritage in the Post-Abbasid Period* with Cambridge Scholars Publishing, came out in 2019.

Jennifer Schneider is an educator, attorney, and writer. Her work appears in *The Coil*, *The Write Launch*, *Anti-Heroin Chic*, *The Popular Culture Studies Journal*, *unstamatic*, *One Sentence Stories*, and other literary and scholarly journals.

Lana Spendl's chapbook, *We Cradled Each Other in the Air*, is available from Blue Lyra Press. Her short stories, essays, and poems have appeared in *The Rumpus*, *New Ohio Review*, *The Greensboro Review*, *Zone 3*, *Baltimore Review*, *Denver Quarterly*, *Hobart*, and other journals. She lives in Bloomington, Indiana, where she is working on a collection of short fiction.